PRINCIPAL PEER EVALUATION

We dedicate this book
to all of the students in our district,
where each child is an individual of great worth.
Without them, this book would have little meaning.

PRINCIPAL PEER EVALUATION

Promoting Success From Within

Libia S. Gil

CORWIN PRESS, INC.
A Sage Publications Company
2455 Teller Road
Thousand Oaks, CA 91320-2218

E-mail: order@corwinpress.com
Call: (800) 818-7243   Fax: (800) 4-1-SCHOOL
www.corwinpress.com

For information:

Corwin Press, Inc.
A Sage Publications Company
2455 Teller Road
Thousand Oaks, California 91320
E-mail: order@corwinpress.com

Sage Publications Ltd.
6 Bonhill Street
London EC2A 4PU
United Kingdom

Sage Publications India Pvt. Ltd.
M-32 Market
Greater Kailash I
New Delhi 110 048 India

Printed in the United States of America

Library of Congress Cataloging-in-Publication Data

Gil, Libia.
    Principal peer evaluation: Promoting success from within / by Libia
Gil (for the Chula Vista Elementary School District).
        p.   cm.
    Includes bibliographical references (p.   ) and index.
    ISBN 0-7619-7709-0 (c)
    ISBN 0-7619-7710-4 (p)
    1. Elementary school principals—Rating of—California—Chula Vista.
2. Peer review—California—Chula Vista.   3. Chula Vista Elementary
    School District (Chula Vista, Calif.)   I. Chula Vista Elementary School
    District (Chula Vista, Calif.)   II. Title.
LB2831.964.C2 G55   2001
372.12′012—dc21   00-012626

This book is printed on acid-free paper.

01   02   03   04   05   06   07   7   6   5   4   3   2   1

Acquiring Editor:	Robb Clouse
Editorial Assistant:	Kylee Liegl
Production Editor:	Denise Santoyo
Editorial Assistant:	Kathryn Journey
Designer/Typesetter:	Tina Hill
Cover Designer:	Michelle Lee

Contents

List of Figures and Tables

Acknowledgments

We are grateful to all who contributed to the writing of this book. In particular, we appreciate all the principals, assistant superintendents, and board members in the Chula Vista Elementary School District for their interest, participation, and support. Special acknowledgment goes to Kathie Clayson for her assistance in coordinating and typing the manuscript at the last minute, and to Rosemary Craig Barnes, who assisted us in coordinating the writings.

In addition, the contributions of the following reviewers are gratefully acknowledged:

William D. Silky
Oswego State University of New York, Oswego, New York

John Spiesman
Geneva Area Schools, Geneva, Ohio

Deborah R. Alexander
Kingston Elementary School, Kingston, Tennessee

Donald Hackmann
Iowa State University, Ames, Iowa

Karen Tichy
Catholic Education Office, Saint Louis, Missouri

About the Authors

Gretchen Donndelinger (gdonndel@cvesd.k12.ca) is Principal of Castle Park Elementary School in the Chula Vista Elementary School District. She began her education career in 1990 as a third-grade teacher in the Poway Unified School District, received her preliminary administrative credential, and was promoted to assistant principal in 1993. She is active in many community activities, such as the Filipino American Educators of San Diego County, Council of Philippine American Organizations of San Diego County, and the Filipino American National Historical Society. She is currently the president of the Filipino American Educators Association of California. She also belongs to numerous professional organizations, such as the Association of California School Administrators, the Association of American School Administrators, and the National Association of Elementary School Principals. She received her BA from San Diego State University, her

MA from National University, and her PhD from the University of Southern California.

Fred Elliott (felliott@cvesd.k12.ca) is Principal of Discovery Charter School in the Chula Vista Elementary School District. He began his educational career in 1970 in an open-space loft school where he taught with nine other team members, developing and implementing a 5/6 instructional curriculum for the school. He has been a resource teacher and became a principal in 1987. In 1994, he opened a new school, now a California State Charter School, with a focus on standards-based curriculum and foreign language. With the increase of at-risk students and families in stress, he feels it is important as the instructional leader to create a nurturing and supportive school environment that will enhance and develop the critical attributes all children need to become resilient children. Therefore, it is imperative that, as a leader, he takes a strong role as a child advocate to affirm that he can and does make a difference in children's lives.

Bruce Ferguson (bferguso@cvesd.k12.ca) is Principal of Hilltop Drive Elementary School in the Chula Vista Elementary School District and adjunct professor at San Diego State University and National University. He began his educational career in 1990 as a fifth-grade teacher in the San Diego Unified School District. During his tenure, he taught grades K through 6 in all parts of the city and was promoted to assistant principal of Miramar Ranch Elementary School in 1998. He received his BA, teaching credential, and MA from San Diego State University.

Libia S. Gil (lgil@cvesd.k12.ca) has been superintendent of the Chula Vista Elementary School District since 1993. During her tenure, the district has experienced continuous growth, currently serving 22,350 students in 37 schools. She has supported the establishment of five charter schools and fostered the successful implementation of numerous school change models, such as Accelerated Schools, Comer School Development program, as well as forging partnerships with the Edison Schools Project, the School Futures Research Foundation, and the Ball Foundation. She began her teaching career in the Los Angeles Unified School District and has taught in various programs, including English as a

Second Language and Gifted and Talented programs. During her teaching experiences, she and two colleagues created a successful K-to-12 alternative school and numerous alternative classroom programs. She has held a variety of administrative positions, including elementary school principal in the ABC School District and area administrator and assistant superintendent for curriculum and instruction for the Seattle Public Schools. She has a PhD in curriculum and instruction from the University of Washington.

Marjorie Grigsby (mgrigsby@cvesd.k12.ca) is Principal of Loma Verde Elementary School in the Chula Vista Elementary School District. During her tenure, the school has grown from 540 students in 18 classrooms to more than 735 students in more than 30 classrooms. She began her education career in 1964 teaching Grades 3 through 6 in the Bellevue School District in Washington. In 1969, she transferred to the Chula Vista Elementary School District, where she taught fifth/sixth grade until she became a principal in 1993. During her years as a teacher in Chula Vista, she pioneered such concepts as one-space (loft) team teaching and year-round education. She became actively involved in the Program Quality Review process as a lead reviewer and district trainer. In addition, she was assigned site-assistant administrative duties at two separate schools. Active in site development and student learning support, she established focus teams and successfully attained several educational financial support grants. She received her BA from Washington State University, her MA from United States International University, her preliminary administrative credential from National University, and her education services degree from Point Loma Nazarene University.

William Hall (whall@cvesd.k12.ca) is Principal of Kellogg Performing Arts School in the Chula Vista Elementary School District, where he has worked for 31 years. He is also a core adjunct faculty member at National University. He is a 1968 graduate of the University of San Diego with a major in Spanish. As an undergraduate, he was nominated for membership in La Sociedad Naciónal Hispanica, the National Spanish Honor Society. He received his MA in counselor education, also from the University of San Diego. In 1984, he earned his PhD from United States International University.

Vera Madison (vmadison@cvesd.k12.ca) is Principal of Halecrest Elementary School, a science/technology magnet school in the Chula Vista Elementary School District. She has taught primary, intermediate, and upper grades. Her experience includes being a teacher with the Department of Defense overseas, teaching the children of U.S. personnel at Ramstein Air Force Base in Germany for 2 years. She also taught for a year in Okinawa, Japan. Her overseas assignments enabled her to develop insights and understandings regarding many cultures and communities in Europe and Asia, and firsthand multicultural experiences enriched her life and helped her gain an appreciation for all people of the world. She became a certified Miller-Unruh reading teacher and later an elementary school principal. She completed her undergraduate studies at the University of Wisconsin, Whitewater, with a BA in education. She received her MA and PhD in education from United States International University, San Diego. She has been recognized by the community with two PTA Honorary Service Awards.

Bonnie McGrath (bmcgrath@cvesd.k12.ca) is Principal of Finney Elementary School in the Chula Vista Elementary School District. She has been in education for more than 20 years as a classroom teacher, site-level administrator, and district office personnel. She had the fortunate opportunity to train as a Reading Recovery Teacher Leader and to work in the training of adults. She believes that she can affect the lives of more children by working with teachers and adult educators.

Jorge A. Ramirez (jramire2@cvesd.k12.ca) is Director of the Chula Vista Learning Community Charter School, the district's fifth charter school, developed in partnership with School Futures Research Foundation, a position he has held since 1998. He began his administrative career in 1997 as assistant principal of Calvin J. Lauderbach Elementary School in the Chula Vista Elementary School District. He is a national certified trainer in the Micro-Society® Comprehensive School Reform Program and adjunct professor for San Diego State University's Bilingual Teacher Credential Program. He is currently working on his doctorate at the University of San Francisco with an emphasis on international multicultural education.

Pat Roth (proth@cvesd.k12.ca) is Principal of Chula Vista Hills Elementary School in the Chula Vista Elementary School District. Starting her career as a preschool teacher, she had her first teaching experience in a public school in a first/second-grade combination class in the Chula Vista Elementary School District. She was one of the first mentor teachers for Chula Vista and, in 1987, became principal of Hazel Goes Cook Elementary School. During her teaching career, she won the first Teacher of the Year award for the Chula Vista Elementary School District and was also the district's first TRIBES trainer. In addition, she was a certified Orff Music Clinician, has been honored by the San Diego Reading Association as Administrator of the Year, and has served as both president and copresident of the Chula Vista Administrators Association. She is a member of the International Reading Association, the Association of California School Administrators, the National Association of Elementary School Principals, and the Year-Round School Administrators Association. She received a BA in liberal studies, an MA in curriculum and instruction, and an administrative services credential from San Diego State University.

Connie Smith (csmith2@cvesd.k12.ca) is Principal of Juarez-Lincoln Accelerated School in the Chula Vista Elementary School District. She has been an administrator in public school education for more than 15 years. Through her leadership, Juarez-Lincoln implemented the Accelerated Schools reform model through Stanford University in 1994 and was selected as one of two elementary schools in California to become a model technology site, using ISDN and videoconferencing technology across the kindergarten through sixth grade curriculum, earning the school a national and international presence as an Apple Distinguished School. She has extensive experience in California and nationally as a consultant through the Education for the Future Foundation (EFF), presenting workshops on data collection and analysis and the School Portfolio Process. She received an MA in early childhood education from United States International University in 1975 and an additional MA degree from San Diego State University in 1976 in administration and supervision as a Carnegie Fellow.

CORWIN
PRESS

The Corwin Press logo—a raven striding across an open book—represents the happy union of courage and learning. We are a professional-level publisher of books and journals for K–12 educators, and we are committed to creating and providing resources that embody these qualities. Corwin's motto is "Success for All Learners."

Introduction

The challenge of public education today is to increase student achievement. This mandate requires educators to abandon "business as usual" practices. Teachers, principals, parents, and administrators must accept responsibility for improving learning and increasing skills. This mandate demands dramatic changes in how districts are structured; superintendents, board members, and principals must provide leadership for teachers, children, and the community. Principals, in particular, are more accountable today for both process and outcomes at school sites.

Peer evaluation is like a dance: a rhythmic and dynamic event in which everyone can participate at various stages, in tune with external or internal music. The purpose of this book is to describe how this challenge was met in the Chula Vista Elementary School District, the largest kindergarten through sixth grade educational district in the state of California. In a district that embraces 103 square miles between the city of San Diego and the international border between the United States and Mexico, more than 23,000 students attend 37 elementary schools. Of these schools, 21 can be described as traditional calendar schools, 13 as single-track year-

1

round schools, and 3 as extended-year schools. About 40 home languages are spoken in a district that is 62.3% Hispanic.

Change began in Chula Vista in the fall of 1993, as the superintendent conducted interviews with all principals to uncover important issues facing the district. She soon learned that the performance evaluation process for school principals was among the top three concerns in the district.

These early days are described more fully in Chapter 1, "Context for Change," which highlights the historical context for challenging the status quo and moving to a different level of meaningful professional engagement. The superintendent describes a number of specific events that established the foundation for changing traditional practices.

In Chapter 2, "A New Role for the Principal," the genesis of a peer-evaluation concept for principals is described. Although principals were the focus of this change initiative, the primary stimulus for change, as always, was student advocacy. It is not coincidental that a framework for Student-Based Decision Making was developed during the same period, and it is also outlined in this chapter.

The process of establishing a new format for the evaluation process is documented in Chapter 3, "Keep Moving Forward." The development of peer-evaluation groups is described here, and exceptions to this process involving disciplinary situations are also discussed. One principal powerfully describes the professional and personal benefits of peer support.

For school districts seeking a model, crucial information is contained in Chapter 4, "Two Steps Forward, One Step Back: Aren't We There Yet?" The process of creating continuum-based principal performance standards and leadership standards is described, and these standards are defined in some detail. The chapter also describes some of the growing pains experienced by the superintendent and principals.

In Chapter 5, "Lessons Learned and Beyond," we summarize our progress, look ahead to the next steps, examine unresolved challenges, and identify future opportunities that will ultimately fuel our efforts as the leadership role is redefined. This concluding chapter also provides insights from the principals' perspective.

In 1998, as a result of growing national interest in creating alternative evaluation processes for school administrators, Chula Vista Elementary School District Superintendent Libia Gil was invited to write an article for *The School Administrator*. The article, "Principals Evaluating Peers" (see Appendix A), described the early phases in establishing the principal peer-evaluation process and identified its strengths and weaknesses.

The education community responded with requests for additional information. A representative group of 10 principals gathered to think, collaborate, and write about this transformational process. This book is the result of the work of this dedicated group.

The steps taken to redesign the Chula Vista Elementary School include a Shared Vision and Values, strategic goals, Student-Based Decision Making, formation of principal peer groups, development of a continuum model for principal performance evaluations, and the transformation of principals from building managers/program implementers to instructional leaders. The model provides a useful pattern for facilitating the development of the principal's leadership capacity to meet and exceed the challenges for tomorrow's public education.

1 Context for Change

Leadership isn't a title or an entitlement. It is not a right or a gift. It's a decision. You can become an effective school leader if you make up your mind to be.

—Robert D. Ramsey

Successful change requires planning and careful analysis. It is often important that the good elements of the present are retained. A warning against "throwing out the baby with the bath water" is an important and often forgotten maxim. Change agents must be mindful of the need to honor positive, long-held rituals from which an organization gains pride and a sense of community. To neglect these practices or to discard these rituals could send a signal that nothing in the past was good or worthwhile, and such a signal could, in turn, foster unnecessary resentment and resistance toward proposed change initiatives. However, agents of change are often obliged to make tough decisions to move the organization forward. In the context of this book, the change process led to a positive organizational philosophy and framework resulting in districtwide increased student achievement. In *Teaching the Elephant to Dance*, James Belasco (1991) says, "Previous successes and past practices root American and European companies firmly to old ways of doing business. We can count on the fact that the old way of doing business will not succeed in the future" (p. 4). Educational organizations are no exception. Long-held beliefs concerning traditional school district organizational models do not support the expectations placed on today's school principal. The Policy Forum on Educational Leadership states, "The hallmark of effective principals is that they concentrate on improving teaching and learning" (Black, 2000). What are the elements of an organizational structure that supports this essential component of a contemporary learning environment?

SETTING THE STAGE

Planned change begins with a thorough assessment of the current state of the organization and the community. Change agents are cautioned to carefully assess the present and identify all stakeholders. In a school district, this assessment phase may include meetings and forums with principals, teachers, students, parents, employee organizations, business leaders, the Chamber of Commerce, community organizations including senior citizens' groups, private schools, neighboring school districts, religious organizations, and city government. One method of gathering ideas and opinions to learning firsthand is by conducting a series of community forums. The information gathered from these contacts supports the development of an action plan. Additional assessment techniques may include an independent curriculum audit to examine all instructional and support systems throughout a district. The final step in setting the stage for change involves a district-level strategic planning process. Together, information from all groups is used to create a shared vision, identify values and beliefs, and set the goals for all students in the district.

In Chula Vista, California, the outcome of an in-depth current state assessment by the newly selected superintendent led to a shared vision as described above. The work of these groups is illustrated in Figures 1.1 and 1.2.

In the fall of 1993, the superintendent conducted an assessment of the Chula Vista Elementary School District. Each of the principals was interviewed and provided insights on strengths and areas for districtwide improvement. The principals' performance evaluation process quickly surfaced on the list of the top three issues. A strong majority shared the view that the existing evaluation process was a

Figure 1.1. Chula Vista Elementary School District: Our Shared Vision

The Chula Vista Elementary School District is committed to providing a successful, safe, challenging, and nurturing educational experience, while promoting the joy and importance of learning for all our children.

Our children are high-achieving, innovative thinkers. They are multiliterate, self-reliant, and confident. They have a lifelong love of learning and are socially responsible citizens. The district takes pride in developing each child's full potential, while recognizing his or her uniqueness.

We value and find strength in our diversity. Learning is meaningful and relevant; is connected with each child's individual needs, ethics, culture, and experiences; and is linked with the world outside the classroom.

Families, staff, and our entire community are full partners actively working in a collaborative manner for the benefit of each child's education. Together, we have an investment in our district's vision and believe a child's success equals our success. We ensure an environment in which everyone is valued and treated with dignity and respect. Everyone assumes responsibility for the success of the school community.

The entire educational community accepts the challenge of change and is motivated to acquire skills and values for a rapidly changing world. We create dynamic learning experiences by supporting and encouraging excellent teaching and the educational growth of family and staff.

The Chula Vista Elementary School District community is dedicated to instilling hope for the future so that today's children will share their vision with future generations.

—Adopted by Board of Education, March 21, 1995

"dog-and-pony show" with little or no relevance to leadership, performance, or student achievement. Under the process used at that time, principals annually presented individual school goals and objectives to a panel consisting of the superintendent, assistant superintendents, and other management staff. Individual principals felt compelled to "jump through hoops" to please central office administrators, with little or no accountability for leadership's impact on staff and student performance. There was no continual inquiry process linking leadership skills to efforts at the site. Some principals were

---

Figure 1.2. Chula Vista Elementary School District: Our Shared Values

---

Equality

We believe each child is an individual of great worth entitled to develop to his or her full potential. All children can and will learn, and deserve equal access to a quality education.

Equity

We believe there is no significant difference in educational outcomes based on race, gender, or economic status. Solutions, resources, programs, services, and support are applied in a manner which develops the full potential of each child.

Accountability

We value and recognize individuals who assume responsibility for and demonstrate commitment and dedication to serving the interests of all children.

Ethical Responsibility

We value each individual who practices, teaches, and serves as a role model of dignity, respect, honesty, integrity, and trust.

Diversity

We seek, encourage, and respect each individual's contributions and value a multicultural perspective.

Teamwork

We believe that families are the primary role models for our children. We are committed to teamwork and collaboration to provide maximum services for students, staff, and community. This partnership among families, community, and schools is the foundation of our children's educational success.

Innovation

We are committed to challenging the status quo and embracing a technological world.

Excellence

We are committed to high standards of performance throughout the district and continuously seek and utilize new knowledge and skills.

—Adopted by Board of Education, March 21, 1995

---

frustrated and discouraged with the lack of a meaningful role in making critical decisions. A traditional top-down directive approach left many principals describing a void in communication and a feeling of exclusion from the decision-making process. Principals said they were the last to learn about decisions and outcomes.

> Most transformation programs satisfy themselves with shifting the same old furniture about in the same old room. Some seek to throw some of the furniture away. But real transformation requires that we redesign the room itself. Perhaps even blow up the old room. It requires that we change the thinking behind our thinking—literally, that we learn to rewire our corporate brains.
>
> *Danah Zohar (Dufour & Eaker, 1992)*

Subsequently, an external team of key educational professionals conducted a curriculum management audit that consisted of a systematic review of policy documents, decision-making processes, and practices. This team made a series of observations and conducted numerous interviews to determine the extent of resource-management alignment with instructional focus and student achievement. Their conclusions confirmed concerns with status quo operations and generated a sense of urgency to redefine roles and functions for the central office staff as well as site leadership. This strengthened the need to recreate the organizational culture, moving from a paternalistic model of "do as I say and I will take care of you" to an accountability focus of "take responsibility for doing what is in the best interest of all children."

> The goals and outcomes we expect for our children are non-negotiable, but how we get there can be flexible and varied. We must recognize that there is no one model or one program that meets the needs of all children. Principals must facilitate powerful teams of staff and parents to create a unique learning environment for each child.
>
> *Superintendent, Chula Vista Elementary School District*

TAKING A CUE FROM BUSINESS

Lessons from the private business sector clearly show the relationship between a successful business and customer satisfaction. The most significant role in transforming the words of the Shared Vision and Values into action for children belongs to the school principal. The accountability-based principal's role substitutes community leader for the traditional role of building administrator. The principal of a school has the opportunity to serve students and parents as customers. When a school district culture is redefined toward self-responsibility and accountability, the principal is positioned to foster unique relationships with the community and staff. With shared goals, philosophy, and empowerment, the principals lay the foundation for implementing successful change efforts. The role of the principal is critical to this new customer service-oriented model. A reorganization of the power structure becomes necessary to give principals not only the responsibility for the operation of the school but also the power to make decisions based on the needs of their school community. This change does not negate the role of superintendent and board but places accountability and school-community decisions at the local level. It encourages dialogue among administration, board, principals, parents, and the community to redefine a healthier and productive educational environment.

A UNIFIED MOVEMENT

Figure 1.3 represents the traditional organizational model, and Figure 1.4 represents the new organizational model of operation currently in place in the Chula Vista Elementary School District. In the traditional model, principals have many hoops to jump through. This model leads to potentially unhealthy coping strategies to circumvent the traditional power structure of directors, coordinators, and even assistant superintendents to get things done. In the traditional model, rather than having the principal and district leaders function as a team, the relationship between the principal and central office focuses on an "us-versus-them" mentality. The people who get things done for their schools are masters of personality and persuasion rather than of professional skill and expertise. In the world of personality and persuasion, preferential relationships create unequal

Figure 1.3. Traditional Organization

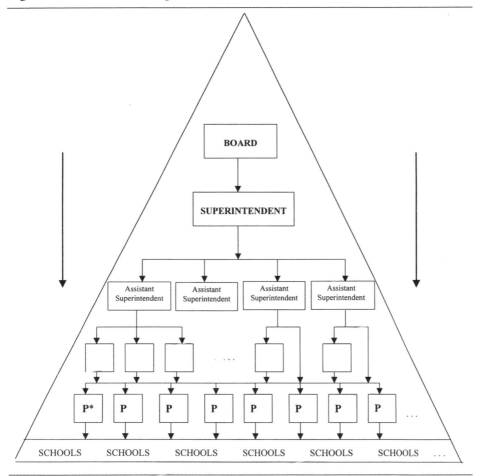

NOTE: *Principal.

treatment and allocation of services. This does little more than per-
petuate the status quo. As new principals come into the district, they
may encounter seemingly insurmountable obstacles because of their
unfamiliarity with the means to get things because they do not know
how to court favors.

The new organizational model (Figure 1.4) inverts the pyramid
and clearly places the focus on parents, students, and the community,
with the principal as the key link between the school and the district.
The principal is now engaged and involved in discussion and decisions. Rather than a culture of primarily top-down decisions, the new

Figure 1.4. Current Organization

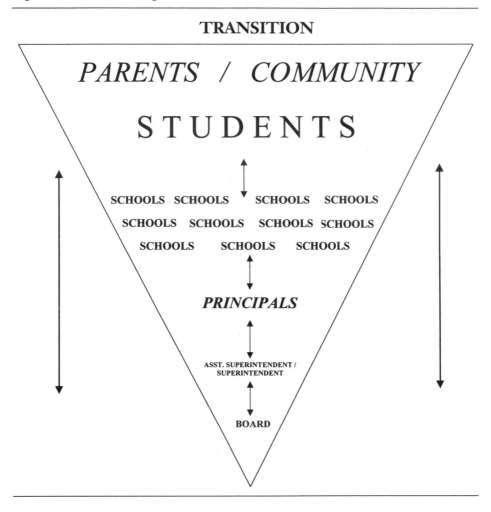

model illustrates the accountability of the principal to know the school, to understand student and community issues, to communicate them as necessary, and to make decisions based on the shared vision. The new model represents a context of collaboration, communication, and parent and community involvement between the district and principals.

Implementing a change based on accountability and shared vision and executing a strategic plan may necessitate some or all of the following structural and philosophical changes:

- All principals, their staff, and their community share the same vision.

- Principals report directly to the superintendent.

- The mission of all central office departments is to support the efforts of school sites (not the reverse).

- All divisions are renamed "Service and Support" to reflect their primary responsibility.

- Principals have authority and accountability for the success of their students.

- The performance expectation is to operate from an internal rather than an external locus of control (operating from a set of core beliefs).

- "We are the district" is a key concept. Principals, as well as all district personnel, are responsible for the success of all children at all schools.

- Structures must be created to support the new dance: Build on strengths, collaborate, and establish a process for continuous critical feedback.

By adopting the guidelines identified above, the infrastructure is established for a new shift. This opens the door for the creation of a principal peer-performance evaluation process.

STEPS TOWARD REDESIGN

The traditional principal-evaluation model addresses management performance categories but does not emphasize the need for changing *leadership* expectations. Setting different performance expectations demands that other systems be reevaluated and revised. The current literature describes many peer-evaluation and coaching models for teachers. None describes the critical components required to support the development of instructional leaders. Concepts, processes, and instruments used in teacher peer evaluation in

Louisville, Kentucky; Seattle, Washington; and Vancouver, Washington, created the initial foundation for Chula Vista's model.

Leadership is vision to see beyond the obvious to the cherished goal. Courage to take the difficult path and stay on course. Energy to keep all the balls in the air and moving. Passion to implement the vision and demand the best. Heart to lead with compassion.

Principal, Chula Vista Elementary School District

2

A New Role
for the Principal

The Boss says, "Go!" The Leader says, "Let's go!"
—Ted Pollock

Major changes, including district reorganization, occurred as each school principal became accountable for student achievement and success of his or her school. Many central office personnel were reassigned, and some positions were eliminated. Several departments were consolidated. The reorganization of the district and the redefinition of the role of the central office departments and personnel permitted a shift of resources to provide support and services to students.

The role of the principal changed from implementing central office mandates to decision making based on collaboration with all stakeholders, always with the needs of the students in mind. The concept of "site-based decision making" was introduced and became the new mode of operation.

Site-based decision making assumes that adults who are closest to children make decisions in the best interest of students. However, in reality, merely shifting decision making from one level to another does not guarantee that student interests take priority over adult

---

Figure 2.1. Student-Based Decision Making: Essential Questions

---

Improving Student Learning, Ethical Responsibility, and *Involving All Stakeholders* are three principles we work with in the decision-making process. The following essential questions provide guidelines as we apply these principles.

HOW DOES THE DECISION IMPROVE STUDENT LEARNING?
- Rationale or evidence that it makes a difference for all children
- Support our vision statement

IS THE DECISION ILLEGAL, UNETHICAL, OR IMMORAL?
- Support our values statement

IS THERE ADVERSE IMPACT ON OTHERS?
- Collaboration with staff, parents, community
- Data collection/research
- District included in problem-solving process
- Fiscal and personnel impact

HOW ARE INDIVIDUAL NEEDS BALANCED WITH GROUP NEEDS?
- Equity

—Adopted by Board of Education, May 19, 1998

---

interests. A clearer and more purposeful framework results when the word *student* is substituted for the word *site*. Today, the concept of *Student-Based Decision Making* is the central focus. This reminds everyone that all decisions must be made in the best interest of students. Along with the district's shared vision and values, guidelines for Student-Based Decision Making were developed and shared with community organizations and all schools.

Figure 2.1 lists some essential questions for Student-Based Decision Making. Principals, administrators, and the community are expected to use these guidelines in all aspects of school-related decisions. If a decision is good for the children, then it is considered.

Some traditional principals had a difficult time adjusting to this new decision-making process. In the Student-Based Decision Making model, emphasis is placed on facilitation skills. Consensus is used to support school or student success. This change in procedural and expected behavior is not comfortable for some. Now, the principal is expected to collaborate with all members of the school community as well as demonstrate commitment to shared decision making. Principals have the freedom to use their creative skills to develop innovative programs to benefit students. Those who embrace this approach are the risk takers who are initiating changes for the purpose of increasing student achievement. The traditionalists tend to be implementers who rely on directives and who value compliance. Most principals enthusiastically accept the change.

> I have always been interested in what is out there, so I don't find the changes personally difficult. I do find I can be impatient when others are not interested in change when it seems so obvious to me why the changes are important and in the best interests of children.
>
> *Principal, Chula Vista Elementary School District*

The skills now required to lead a school successfully displace or modify those used in the traditional model. Dealing with change that results in customer satisfaction means principals must shift roles from authoritarian leader to collaborative leader. Parent, community, and staff involvement becomes a high priority in addressing educational issues. Principals must be willing to invite others to share their ideas and to be avid listeners. Building trust within the entire school community becomes extremely important, as role change and school reform are sustained. The vision of the revitalized educational program more accurately addressing the needs of children begins to actualize itself.

> I feel the paradigm shift has required me to be a more dynamic and effective leader. This process has required me to evaluate and reflect on my role as a leader and change agent.
>
> *Principal, Chula Vista Elementary School District*

AUTHORITARIAN TO COLLABORATOR

As the principal takes on a collaborative leadership role, the challenge is to form teams of often diverse, multiskilled staff, parents, and community members and bring them together to create change. Facilitation and collaboration skills become important. In the facilitator role, a principal brings together the entire education community of staff, students, and parents, building positive relationships to create teams whose members will work collaboratively toward a shared vision. Leadership styles take on a new look, and procedural questions are raised as the team learns the new framework.

Members might ask the following:

■ What topics/decisions need to involve parents/community?

■ What issues need to involve teachers/staff?

■ When should the principal make the final decision?

■ What procedures are followed when involving others in decision making?

■ What process is used to arrive at a final decision?

■ When do the decisions need to be escalated to a higher level?

The answers to these questions will vary with each individual group and circumstance and with the set of priorities people bring to the experience. The responses to these questions form the basis for the development of a subsequent plan for implementation of action, which will bring about the desired outcomes, solutions, or, in effect . . . change. The principal's responsibility is to set the tone and direction for the team to work successfully together.

Subsequent changes at the school site are apparent when the principal becomes a collaborator and instructional leader. Community forums are held to discuss issues and to receive input from parents and all stakeholders. Parents and community members are invited to be on school and district committees. School Site Councils, Parent Teacher Associations (PTAs), and other groups are kept informed of all issues affecting the welfare of students and the school. Successful leaders master the art of recognizing and harnessing the good ideas of everyone around them.

Figure 2.2. A Principal's New Vision of His Role

In the fifties . . . the Ed Sullivan Show often had some Chinese jugglers on the stage . . . who were masterful at juggling real plates on the ends of long, slender poles (8 to 10 feet long). The "trick" was to begin spinning these plates on each stick . . . then [balance] them either on the hand, the finger, the shoulder, the nose, the chin, the forehead, etc. All at the same time! At the apex of this theatrical feat, one plate juggler would have 10 to 11 long poles balanced on some part and/or appendage of his body, with a plate spinning at the top of *each* pole! It was awe-inspiring to watch! *That* is leadership! The key to success is keeping your eye on *every* "plate" . . . making sure it is "spinning" . . . while balancing the "poles," precariously, throughout the juggling display. Concentrate *too much* on one plate . . . and others will come crashing to the floor! Just enough spin on each . . . so when you have *all* of them balanced, the collective dishware will be spinning in unison.

PROGRAM MANAGER TO CHANGE AGENT

Historically, the central office mandated school programs, and the principal's role was merely that of building manager and program implementer. A redesign of the organization now places the principal in the role of change agent and instructional leader. In this participatory model, sites have more autonomy to make decisions based on the unique needs of students. Many decisions are made at the school site. Principals are given the responsibility of facilitating change while increasing student achievement. Effective principals have facilitation and communication skills. They energize people to take action and achieve a common goal. Leadership is a dynamic process, requiring principals and school administrators to be continuous and reflective learners. The process is important but must also be linked to results. To understand the change process is to understand that change creates discomfort and conflict. Listening and mediation skills are essential as the principal/leader works with individuals through the change process.

The need to make decisions quickly and efficiently is continuously pressing on the school principal. In reality, the role of principal/leader often involves a balancing act, with events constantly unfolding at a relentless pace. One principal visualizes this role change as described in Figure 2.2.

The need for long-term strategic planning and reform rather than "quick fixes" has significant implications for both schools and principals. It is necessary for principals to see themselves as advocates for changing conditions to promote student learning. This is a major behavioral shift for many principals. Principals react in a variety of ways depending on their ability to manage change, both personally and professionally. Principals, as change agents and leaders, are reminded to take caution as they sift through the myriad solutions available to ensure that all efforts are focused, purposeful, and beneficial to the children.

> Given these facts, concentration is the secret to success—one idea, one goal, one dream.
>
> *Author Unknown*

BUILDING MANAGER TO INSTRUCTIONAL LEADER

The transformation of the principal in today's public education setting is one that mirrors the trends of society as seen in history. Table 2.1 was constructed from ideas from Schlechty's (1990) book, *Schools for the 21st Century*. It illustrates the concept of how past history plays a role in shaping public education today.

The response to societal cries is, in fact, what defines the focus of the school. The principal is the choreographer of the vision, role, structure, and purpose, if school reform is to increase student achievement. Public school administrators must meet the needs of society if they are indeed going to be successful.

CURRENT STATE OF CHANGE

The new model transforms the role of the principal from an administrator who controls and maintains the status quo to an instructional leader. The principal now concentrates on creating a collaborative approach involving students, parents, and teachers. The school com-

TABLE 2.1
Historical Changes in the Role of the Principal

Era	Focus of School	Role of the Principal
Civil War	Promote republican/morality and civic duty	Chief priest
Post-Civil War	Americanize immigrants and fit into urban factory system	Manager of the industrial center Effective time manager
Late 19th century	Serve social reform's political, economic, and cultural ends imposed on children	Equalizer of pain and suffering One who remedies social ills
Early-mid 20th century	Serve as an engine of social reform	
Late 20th century	Prepare students for the era of technology	Visionary
Present	Standards, accountability	Instructional leader

munity becomes actively involved in short- and long-term decisions as a result of the principal's role change. The community's voices become stronger as members embark on the change process. In fact, individual voices become stronger because *every* member provides value to decisions.

New roles promote each principal's personal and professional growth. New skills and understandings develop. Skills include the ability not only to manage a school building but to be the instructional leader who ensures student academic success. Principals seek out and draw on a myriad of resources supporting the teaching/ learning process. They must analyze pertinent data to determine specific needs of students and community, plan a deliberate course of action, and successfully implement necessary changes. The new model also requires each principal to operate from an internal rather than external locus of control, to operate from core beliefs and values.

This change in focus is the genesis of a peer-evaluation model. It provides the groundwork for administrators to collaborate and communicate with one another as they define the steps needed to change. Peer groups provide an ideal arena for group reflection among principals. Senge (1999) refers to "an effective learning organization" as one that creates a reflective environment in which people have a habit of regularly taking time to think about how things are going and how they might be improved. He states that many worthwhile change initiatives wither because they were not nourished by collective reflections. Collective reflection allows people in an organization to think "outside the box" and imagine new ways to solve problems (Frase, Downey, & Canciamilla, 1999). The principal peer-group process creates the environment for this to occur.

My role as a leader is to first educate myself by keeping up with current research and best practices. Second, in addition to leader/manager, I must serve as head cheerleader at the site. This includes keeping a positive attitude and modeling behavior I want to see manifested by staff, students, and parents. Most important, I am the keeper of the vision and must stay on focus.

Principal, Chula Vista Elementary School District

3

Keep Moving Forward

If you can't stand the heat, get out of the kitchen.
—Harry Truman

The redesign of the Chula Vista Elementary School District and the establishment of a new vision and values, strategic goals, and Student-Based Decision Making framework enabled a small volunteer group of principals to begin the process of developing the new evaluation process. As designing began, considerable time was spent defining the purpose of an evaluation. The design team agreed that the primary purpose of an evaluation process was to promote professional and personal growth and development. The team further agreed that an effective evaluation process would be ongoing and would reflect an open and honest communication approach with immediate critical feedback to avoid surprises.

The practice of conducting multiple assessments during performance evaluation is applicable to adults, as well as to students. Regular customer satisfaction surveys of community, parents, staff, and students are conducted, and feedback is seriously considered and incorporated into improvement action plans. Longitudinal student-achievement data, as well as attendance rates and other school profile

---

Figure 3.1. Questions for Principal Self-Reflection

What significant impact have I made on student achievement?

Is it adequate or satisfactory?

If it is good, is "good" enough?

---

data, are incorporated into the feedback process. Multiple sources of data are used in addition to Student-Based Decision Making (see Chapter 2).

Even though all educational leaders can recite the common attributes needed by students to succeed in the new millennium—critical thinking; problem solving; teamwork; and ability to embrace change, ambiguity, and diversity—the question remains, How will our students acquire these attributes if adults do not model them? If we expect higher performance for students and staff members, we need to start with ourselves. Basic questions for self-reflection are found in Figure 3.1. These questions sustain focus on the student and student achievement.

A major change in values and expectations contributes to a wide range of reactions. Leaders who grasp the implications are also those who understand application, adaptability, and the need to change. Those who are not able to analyze or reflect, and who are unable to see the significance in shifting role and responsibility, will continue to wander in the past and are at risk of becoming anchors of resistance (see Table 3.1). Principals are expected to embrace and integrate the shared vision and values in this district.

PEER-EVALUATION EXCEPTIONS

Successful peer-evaluation processes function with teamwork and a high trust level. Trust is the cornerstone of this process, and trust is earned over time. To support professional growth and a collegial atmosphere, peer evaluation has greater success when there are no disciplinary responsibilities. The responsibility for disciplinary interventions is left at the level of the superintendent. In the Chula

TABLE 3.1
Major Values/Expectations Shifts:
Chula Vista Elementary School District Administrators

Traditional Values/Expectations	Current Values/Expectations
Manager	Instructional leader
School administrator	Community leader
Static	Dynamic
Compliance/conformity	Accountability/responsibility
Prescriptive	Ambiguous/creative
Directive	Influential
Adult-focused	Student-focused
Entitlement/longevity	Merit
Status quo	Disequilibrium
Authority	Learner
Buck passer	Problem solver
Ignorant	Data driven
Victim/martyr	Empowered
Complacency	Higher expectations
External locus of control	Internal locus of control
Blame frame	Aim frame

Vista Elementary School District, assistant superintendents are designated as coaches. Patterns of parent, staff, and/or community complaints often lead to regular observations, visitations, and progressive communication with the assistant superintendents and superintendent.

As in any organization, disciplinary situations occur. These may include substance or alcohol abuse; fiscal mismanagement; data fabrication; threats of physical or verbal abuse toward staff, parents, and/or students; AWOL (absent from school site without notification and/or authorization); falsification of documents; discrimination; and other violations of legal and ethical standards. Examples of each of these categories may represent one-time events or patterned behavior.

Obviously, the consequences for each situation depend on the circumstances of the violation and the individual response. Sanctions may range from conferences and documentation to suspension from duties and immediate removal.

In this district, "plans for improvement" or "assistance plans for change" are initiated when the superintendent determines that the action is necessary. During this process, the individual meets with the superintendent and an assistant superintendent on a regular basis for goal setting, monitoring, coaching, and getting feedback. During these sessions, principals may elect to bring a peer-group representative to the conference sessions. Peer-group support is often instrumental in helping individuals to strengthen leadership behaviors. Peer support is also valuable in clarifying communications. However, it is ultimately the individual's decision. The superintendent and assistant superintendents respect confidentiality for all personnel matters. As trust deepens, the strength and support of the peer group mature, and personal and professional growth occurs.

The following personal account illustrates the strength of the peer group, the support peers may offer, and the importance in placing discipline outside the peer group.

ONE PRINCIPAL'S JOURNEY—A CASE STUDY

In October 1997, I was asked to meet with the superintendent regarding my role as a leader. In the time between this notice and the actual meeting, I went through a period of self-reflection and second-guessing. I entered the meeting with trepidation and not knowing exactly what was in store for me.

During the course of the initial meeting with the superintendent, I was asked to develop an improvement plan that would focus on changes in leadership behavior—not just activities. It was suggested that I meet with assistant superintendents. The assistance of a visiting doctoral candidate/superintendent's intern was also made available to me. At that time, a series of biweekly meetings was scheduled with the superintendent. The purpose of these meetings was to provide updates on my action plan and receive feedback. The method used for feedback was that of inquiry, causing me to self-reflect. My reactions during this process mirrored those of my colleagues as mentioned in Chapter 4 through the development of principal standards. I spent a great deal of time asking myself, What does she (the superintendent) want? What do they (the cabinet) want? I have always been a team player and dedicated to my profession. "Tell me what you want and I will do it." It soon became obvious that this tactic was not working.

It was at this point that I knew I would need the help of my peers if I was going to survive both emotionally and professionally. This was one of the most devastating and challenging periods of my life. It caused me to question my leadership ability and my very identity. I went through periods of despair, anger, and self-doubt. On the practical side, my financial security was at risk. At the lowest point of this process, I was asked by the superintendent what I could say and, more important, do to convince her I should remain in my position as a principal. Despite all my questioning and self-doubt, I was convinced of one thing . . . I would not give up. I would do whatever it took to change. She was able to detect a new level of confidence and commitment that convinced her I would succeed.

I contacted several principals (both in and outside my peer group) who had expertise in areas I wanted to strengthen. Their advice and assistance was invaluable. Most significant was the fact that I felt comfortable reaching out for help. Trust levels had been established, and lines of communication opened within and between peer groups that empowered me.

In July 1998, I attended the Principal's Academy at the Child Development Center, Yale University, where I learned about the Comer School Development Process. This was a Gestalt for me—I got the big picture. I found a mechanism which would be a unifying factor, which was the missing link at the school, and which was philosophically aligned with our belief that student achievement would be positively impacted by strengthening families and the surrounding community. I also found the answer to the question I (and many of my colleagues) had been asking: What does she want? It wasn't about determining what someone else expects (do as I say and I will take care of you). It was about knowing myself through self-reflection and developing an internal locus of control. When I quit worrying about pleasing others and focused on doing what was best for children and my school, I had reached a turning point. In February 1999, I was formally released from the Assistance Plan and recognized for the inner strength and insight it took to successfully move through this process.

CABINET PERSPECTIVES

The principal evaluation process evolved from assistant superintendent and superintendent as the sole evaluators, to principals forming groups to redesign their evaluation process. In the traditional model,

---

Figure 3.2. A Cabinet Member's Perspective of the Principal Peer-Evaluation Process

---

The principal evaluation process has become more reflective, moving from extrinsic to intrinsic leadership. The emphasis is on multiple levels of communication and ultimately greater accountability for results.

A cultural shift is happening in our district. The role of central administration is to support principal growth as lifelong learners. When a principal shows initiative toward excellence, there should be rewards for going above and beyond, the ultimate goal being to build site capacity to make an impact on staff and students.

Principal standards, peer evaluation, and our entire system of accountability (vision, values, student-based decision making) flourishes when we pull together with unity and common purpose. Weaker leaders are strengthened, and strong leaders are further empowered. The status quo leaves individuals and the student-centered goals at risk of failure. This process moves us forward with confidence and strength. Talent is built on the strengths of the team!

---

the assistant superintendent shares the responsibility of coaching and facilitating leadership development. In this district, the cabinet is made up of the assistant superintendents and the superintendent. Figure 3.2 relates one cabinet member's perspective on the evolution of the principal peer-evaluation process.

BOARD PERSPECTIVES

The Chula Vista Elementary School District Board has a history of teamwork and unity in its focus on children first. Significant changes occurred in the policies and practices of the district because of the board's leadership.

Board members voice a common concern about the need for dynamic school leadership and their expectation that the superintendent will hold people accountable for higher performance. The following statements reflect the board members' views on peer evaluation and principal performance standards.

With the current climate of accountability facing public schools, we must have real accountability at all levels of the educational system. Comprehensive evaluation processes are at the core of true accountability. I have long felt that our evaluation process for administrators in the district was inadequate. Peer evaluation, when truly embraced as a growth process for everyone involved, as opposed to just an opportunity to pat each other on the back, can be a powerful component of a comprehensive evaluation process.

Peer evaluation will allow a wider view of performance and interaction. . . . If we ultimately achieve an evaluation system that works in a way that gives constant feedback to the person being evaluated so s/he knows when s/he is not being successful, . . . s/he can reflect and make choices about improving what s/he does, or choose a different line of work . . . that would be a great system. Peer review will only work if honest feedback is given to participants even when it is hard to do.

As a board member, I am in full support of a peer-evaluation process for our site administrators. In an environment of trust, a peer evaluation can be a nonthreatening dialogue between two professionals striving to examine and enhance their leadership. Improved leadership is a powerful tool to improve student performance.

The difference between a leader and a manager will become glaringly apparent as the district moves forward with the implementation of the principal standards and peer evaluation.

Board member

Two Steps Forward, One Step Back: Aren't We There Yet?

4

Just when you see the light at the end of the tunnel, someone adds more tunnel.

—Dr. Jim Benson (Dufour & Eaker, 1991, p. 218)

One of the next steps in redesign is the formation of peer groups. Peer groups initially formed through self-selection with consideration for common goals, geographic representation, size, diversity, and relationships. Peer-groups range in size from four to seven members, and groups meet regularly throughout the school year. Subsequent groups are organized heterogeneously.

Principals have an initial conference with the superintendent followed by group goal-setting sessions with their peer groups. The groups select a common focus based on predetermined criteria. The peer groups use performance indicators in professional growth, school improvement, evaluation of school personnel, management, communication, and community relations. Throughout this process, individual concerns or personnel issues remain confidential between the principal and the superintendent and/or assistant superintendents unless the principal chooses to share this information.

> Significant change takes from 7 to 10 years. Within the last 6 years, principals have moved from having evaluation done to them to having an active voice as the evaluation process continues to evolve. The cycles of change, storming, forming, norming, and conforming continue to be evident as this process evolves.
>
> *Michael Fullan (Ramsey, 1999)*

Individuals are evaluated by peer groups on a 2-year rotation cycle. New principals are evaluated annually for a 3-year probationary period. The implementation of peer groups does not preclude the superintendent's role and responsibility in holding individuals accountable for their leadership behaviors and implementing plans for improvement when necessary.

Peer groups use an array of approaches to observe, learn, and provide feedback to each other. These include classroom observations, analysis of student work, formal interviews with key staff and parent leaders, and regular meetings to solve problems and exchange ideas. Peer sessions also provide a measure of catharsis.

Principals assess the strengths and weaknesses of the peer group evaluation process. Among reported strengths are

- Valued interactions with other principals, which lead to new relationships and friendships

- Support and assistance in dealing with difficult issues

- Diverse perspectives and varied expertise

- Brainstormed solutions to common and uncommon problems

- Trust built through frequent nonthreatening, candid communication with a core group

- Meaningful evaluation established through learning and cooperative efforts

> **BOX 4.1**
>
> **Group Conferences**
>
> **At the end of the first year, group conferences with the superintendent addressed these two questions:**
>
> > **What did we learn?**
> >
> > **What difference was made, if any, on my leadership ability to improve student learning?**

Principals point to these weaknesses: lack of adequate time to visit and process information and reluctance to offer honest, critical feedback of a peer.

Two suggestions that were offered for improving the peer-review process were the need to clearly articulate expectations among group members and to designate one meeting per month for principal peer groups to share procedures among one another. Principals found themselves in the process of change whether or not they wanted to be there. Providing positive support for the change process is critical. Those who resist change require peer and superintendent coaching, and a decision regarding acceptance of the new model or location of a more comfortable traditional model of organization.

The need to change comes as a surprise for some principals. Those who have been in the public school setting for a number of years and have been part of a number of transformational efforts may question and even fear another change process. The perception of new accountability and leadership is colored by the lens of past experience. This causes some to question the need and even the wisdom of going through another transformational process. Agreement is essential: The time for exclusively top-down decision making has come to an end.

PIONEERING THE
PEER EVALUATION PROCESS

In Chapter 1, reference is made to the dearth of research-based material related to peer evaluation and school principals. The Chula Vista principals found that *they* were the pioneers. There are other building models for leadership accountability, but none encompass the elements of peer evaluation with superintendent-cabinet evaluation and potential merit-pay incentives.

MOVING TOWARD PRINCIPAL PERFORMANCE STANDARDS

The Principals' Chula Vista Assistance Team (CHAT) program was established to provide instructional leadership training aligned with the CHAT teacher-training program for new teachers.

The CHAT program affects student learning by increasing teacher effectiveness through a training and assistance program for new teachers. Assistance activities range from monitoring progress to providing ongoing coaching, training, and mentoring. This program provides guidance, monitoring, and assessment of new teachers' progress based on the California Standards for the Teaching Profession (see Figure 4.1).

The Principal CHAT model is designed to recognize peer expertise for instructional leadership with focus on building principals' capacity to mentor and support each other. Two CHAT principal facilitators established regular opportunities for principals to view video teaching and critique lessons based on the California Standards for the Teaching Profession, followed by paired observations at school sites. These principal facilitators subsequently assisted the group in developing the Principal Standards, and they continue to facilitate activities designed to nurture honest collaboration and reflection among principals. These activities are centered around instruction, with the goal of improving student achievement. This emphasis on the development of principals' skills as instructional leaders prompted questions regarding principal evaluations.

PREPARING FOR A TRIAL RUN

Toward the end of the 1997–1998 school year, a committee was formed to research principal evaluation models connected to merit pay. After extensive discussion, research, and many meetings, a recommendation was developed to implement a merit pay system. The

Figure 4.1. California Standards for the Teaching Profession

Engaging and Supporting All Students in Learning
- Connecting students' prior knowledge, life experience, and interests with learning goals
- Using a variety of instructional strategies and resources to respond to students' diverse needs
- Facilitating learning experiences that promote autonomy, interaction, and choice
- Engaging students in problem solving, critical thinking, and other activities that make subject matter meaningful
- Promoting self-directed, reflective learning for all students

Creating and Maintaining Effective Environments for Student Learning
- Creating a physical environment that engages all students
- Establishing a climate that promotes fairness and respect
- Promoting social development and group responsibility
- Establishing and maintaining standards for student behavior
- Planning and implementing classroom procedures and routines that support student learning
- Using instructional time effectively

Understanding and Organizing Subject Matter for Student Learning
- Demonstrating knowledge of subject matter content and student development
- Organizing curriculum to support student understanding of subject matter
- Interrelating ideas and information within and across subject matter areas
- Developing student understanding through instructional strategies that are appropriate to the subject matter
- Using materials, resources, and technologies to make subject matter accessible to students

Planning Instruction and Designing Learning Experiences for All Students
- Drawing on and valuing students' backgrounds, interests, and developmental learning needs
- Establishing and articulating goals for student learning
- Developing and sequencing instructional activities and materials for student learning
- Designing short-term and long-term plans to foster student learning
- Modifying instructional plans to adjust for student needs

Assessing Student Learning
- Establishing and communicating learning goals for all students
- Collecting and using multiple sources of information to assess student learning
- Involving and guiding all students in assessing their own learning
- Using the results of assessments to guide instruction
- Communicating with students, families, and other audiences about student progress

Developing as a Professional Educator
- Reflecting on teaching practices and planning professional development
- Establishing professional goals and pursuing opportunities to grow professionally
- Working with communities to improve professional practices
- Working with families to improve professional practices
- Working with colleagues to improve professional practices
- Balancing professional responsibilities and maintaining motivation

reaction from the group was overwhelmingly negative. Many principals shared a concern that if merit pay were to be instituted, it should be for the teachers, not just principals. Many felt that competition between principals and teachers would produce factions among the team members. The end of the school year delayed further discussion of this aspect of the evaluation process.

When principal peer groups met at the beginning of the 1998–1999 school year, there was continued agitation about the merit pay concept. The superintendent's evaluation discussion with the Board of Education was focused on a more rigorous evaluation process for principals, which would be connected to merit pay. To begin this process, peer-group meetings with the superintendent centered on the roles and responsibilities of principals. Table 4.1 outlines the results of the principal/superintendent discussions. The California Teaching Standards were used to provide a context from which the four domains or areas of focus evolved. These four domains are powerful learning, customer satisfaction, management, and leadership (see Table 4.1 for an overview).

From the four domains, principal leadership behaviors and performance standards were developed in a continuum-based format. Each peer group took responsibility for developing indicators and descriptors based on the four domains. Two weeks later, all principals reviewed their work through a read-around process. The group reached a tenuous consensus following another lengthy read-around session. The format initially included the Beginning, Emerging, Applying, Integrating, and Innovating stages for teacher performance. The principals reviewed these performance standards. Some members traveled in a new direction, some were skeptical but reticent, and others were outright saboteurs. The present continuum format is the result of these group discussions. Merit pay is excluded from this framework.

It is an injustice to pay high-performing and low-performing administrators at the same level.

Board member

TABLE 4.1
Draft, 1998–1999 Chula Vista Elementary School District
Principals' Performance-Based Compensation Plan

Performance Accountability Measures: Developmental Continuum

Powerful Learning

- *Student achievement at grade level*
    - Growth beyond 50th percentile—Multiple Measures
    - Multiple measure indicative of academic growth—John's-BRI, EMI, SAT[9], and SABE
- *Attendance*
    - Meets/exceeds district baseline ('97) percentage
    - Percentage improvement-SARB[a] process
    - Ranking order? incentive program
    - 3% absenteeism
    - 3%-4% max?
    - Percentage of perfect attendance?
- *Discipline/suspensions*
    - District average ('97)–.18%
- *Instructional leadership*
    - CHAT[a] principals—feedback to teacher—outcomes?
- *Technology*
    - Level of implementation plans?
    - Grants written
- *Standards*
    - Integration with curriculum and assessment

Customer Satisfaction

- *Complaints/resolution patterns*
    - Responsiveness, timely communication
- *Gordon Black[a] surveys*
    - Level of improvement?
- *Parent involvement*
    - Number of volunteers
    - Number of parent leaders site/District
    - Quality—how? (narrative)
    - Ways to communicate/solicit input
    - Percentage of parent conferences
    - Parent training opportunities (personal growth)
    - Breakdown of parent ethnicity for school involvement

(Continued)

TABLE 4.1
(Continued)

- *Community involvement*
  - Service organization involvement
  - Partnership number
- *360° survey/review*

Management
- *Personnel evaluation*
  - Honest feedback
  - Substance timeliness/growth/coaching
- *Budget management*
  - Within parameters-carryovers?
  - Over- /underspending
- *Staff development*
  - Focus technology-literacy
- *Teamwork*
  - Unity of purpose, district and site level committee participation
- *Aim frame*[a]
  - Turning negatives to positives
- *Maintenance*
  - Safety/cleanliness—follow-through
  - Pride—sense of welcome
- *Interpersonal relations*

Leadership
- *Visions/values/student-based decision making/goals*
- *Innovative/creative*
- *Flexibility/adaptability*
- *Child advocacy*
  - Diversity
  - Antiracism
  - Inclusion
  - Acceptance of differences
- *Courage*

NOTE: Revised 11/12/98.
a. For explanation of these terms, please see Glossary.
Adapted from the California Commission on Teacher Credentialing and the California Department of Education, 1997, pp. 5-22.

TABLE 4.2
Principal Performance Standards

Leadership Behaviors

Standard 1:   The principal is accountable for staff performance.

Standard 2:   The principal is accountable for building leadership capacity.

Standard 3:   The principal is accountable for customer satisfaction.

Standard 4:   The principal is accountable for acting with integrity and fairness.

Standard 5:   The principal is accountable for managing the school site to be a safe, efficient, and effective learning environment.

FINE-TUNING THE STANDARDS

A subcommittee of three principals accepted the task of revising the elements for the standards. The Interstate School Leaders Licensure Consortium at Illinois State University was helpful in this process, and the following resources were also used: *Proficiencies for Principals*, from the National Association of Elementary School Principals; the Edison Project document for principal evaluation; and the Pueblo Colorado School District No. 60 Administrator Evaluation document. Ideas and language from these documents are found in the standards (see Table 4.2). The language in these documents continues to be refined.

DETOUR

During a review of the redrafted Principal Standards, a vocal cadre of resisters continued to challenge the plan. A recommendation was made to restructure the document to align it with the district's vision, values, strategic goals, and Student-Based Decision Making and to format it with the Pueblo document for principal evaluation. This detoured the group from the originally agreed-on standards format. Many principals supported the change in direction because it appeared to be less cumbersome. For the next several meetings, the sessions were focused in this new direction. When a draft of this new model was shared with the superintendent and cabinet, the latter asked, "What happened to the continuum?" Representatives from the principals' group returned to that group for further discussion. Using this question as an opportunity for reflection, the group reviewed its original purpose.

When this critical question was posed to the principals' group, there was a deep sense of disequilibrium and frustration. Most felt that the new direction was unclear. The dominant questions that surfaced were "What is it that is wanted?" and "Does it really matter what we think or do, when the document will be sent back to us to revise until the cabinet gets the product that it wants?" During these discussions, it was evident that some wanted to go forward, others wanted the superintendent to create the document and give it to them, and still others continued to be totally nonsupportive of any change. After extensive reflection, a decision was made to return to the continuum-based format. The majority of the group supported the development of specific standards that would reflect principal roles and responsibilities. The district's shared vision, values, strategic goals, and Student-Based Decision Making are now embedded in the continuum format of the Principal Standards.

Table 4.2 identifies five leadership standards for all principals. Table 4.3 was the document created to combine the five leadership standards and the district's shared values.

Redesigning any system and implementing change requires tenacity, focus, vision, and energy. Involving all principals is difficult. Day-to-day professional responsibilities at the school site are overwhelming. As in any process, there is continual change and modification. The principals' group is no exception. After multiple drafts, discussion, and sessions, the continuum concept was modified from five to four stages, and these were named Beginning, Emerging, Applying, and Innovating. Several months later, Self-Actualization and Evidence were added. Today, the principals continue to develop the two latter categories. Self-actualization is not necessarily the same for all principals. This leaves the door open to continued personal and professional goals and growth.

TABLE 4.3
Principal Leadership Behaviors

Emotional
Intelligences
Self-Awareness
Self-Regulation
Motivation
Empathy
Social Skills

| | Development, articulation of a *vision* of learning | Nurturing and sustaining a school culture conducive to teaching and learning | Ensure effective *management* of the organization and learning environment | *Collaboration* with family and community members | Acting with *integrity, fairness,* and in an *ethical* manner | Understand and participate in *community* |

	Standards	Benchmark	Activities
Literacy	The principal will provide evidence of continuous student achievement	(1) Use data to ensure success of all students (2) 90% of all students will achieve a minimum of one year's growth (3) Disaggregate local site student achievement (4) Provide quarterly reports that illustrate student achievement	(1) Targeted intervention strategies for identified learners (i.e., RSP, ELL, GATE) (2) Quarterly monitoring of all students: implement intervention strategies—provide professional development
Equity	The principal will develop schoolwide standards-based instructional practices	(1) Implement elements of a standards-based educational program	(1) Align curriculum to standards (2) Develop assessments aligned to standards (3) Examine student work

	Standards	Benchmark	Activities
Collaboration	The principal will demonstrate visionary leadership in assisting staff and parents to increase student achievement	The principal will demonstrate: (1) Cooperation (2) Visibility and effective communication skills (3) Communication of mission/vision/goal (4) Teamwork (5) Effective teacher feedback documentation Utilize district policies, procedures, contractual agreements, and resource people when managing the site and making decisions Staff and site council work collaboratively toward the accomplishment of the district vision and values	
Technology	The principal will (1) Demonstrate uses of technology to effectively manage site data (2) Implement a plan and demonstrate to teachers how to integrate technology into the classroom		
Safe Environment	The principal will develop (1) Safety/discipline plans (2) A plan for conflict management		

MOTIVATION: IT'S ALL IN THE TIMING

During this developmental stage, the superintendent informed several principals that they were being removed from their assignments because of a lack of confidence in their leadership. This event affected the entire principal group. Many perceived that there wasn't a clear process for dismissal and that many colleagues had been unfairly dismissed. This motivated the principals to delineate and objectify performance expectations. The final version of the Principal Standards document is found in Table 4.4. Representatives from each peer group prepared a document for three principals, who had the task of taking the document to the cabinet members for discussion and decision. This document, or its next version, may be used in the future to clearly document performance expectations and outcomes.

REFINING THE PRODUCT

Feedback sessions with the superintendent and cabinet clarified expectations and requirements. By revising the Innovating stage, "above and beyond" behaviors were incorporated. The challenge of developing innovative indicators led us to create the current descriptors and to add the "above and beyond" standard to the Self-Actualization column. The superintendent and cabinet encouraged the entire principal group to continuously challenge their thinking beyond the descriptors currently listed under Innovating. In the course of this work, the phrase "no quacking" was adopted. It serves to send a peer message to members of the group who slip back into old behaviors. One principal provides further explanation.

> Ken Blanchard shared a story at a training seminar for executive principals. This story is one he credits to his friend and fellow author, Wayne Dyer. The setting is a pond where a lively discussion takes place involving the ducks and eagles about what to do as the winter approaches. Now, it really takes Ken Blanchard to tell this story with his rich voice and with the details to set the scene as though you are at the pond observing the action. I can tell you that while the ducks quacked, the winter approached. The eagles, taking flight leaving the snow and cold, looked down on the quacking ducks. The moral of the

(Text continues on page 61)

TABLE 4.4
Standards for Promoting Success From Within

Principal Standard No. 1: The principal is accountable for staff performance that impacts student achievement.

Supervision/Evaluation of Staff

Emerging

- Supervision is performed by administration and in strict compliance with the contract.
- Appropriate forms and documentation are in place.
- All timeline requirements are met.
- In addition to formal and informal supervision by the principal, peer coaching is encouraged, but a well-defined structure for sustained collegial work is not in place.
- There is ongoing dialogue between administration and staff regarding performance in relation to student achievement.
- The principal spends 1 to 2 hours daily doing classroom observations or visitations.

Applying

- Administrators participate in the evaluation process, and their assessments add to a performance portfolio rather than defining it.
- The portfolio includes self and peer assessments, student and parent feedback, and research findings.
- Elements of the SRI Teacher Perceiver that focus on talents and attributes are utilized to provide feedback to staff.
- Through collaboration with the principal, a peer coaching model is clearly developed with well-defined next-step benchmarks in place, which include teachers observing teachers and principal modeling instruction.
- The principal spends 2 to 3 hours in classrooms daily.
- The principal promotes a learning community by establishing staff meetings that focus on research and "Best Practices."

Innovating

- As a way of challenging the status quo, all staff, including the principal, will be evaluated by a representative panel of all stakeholders, including students.
- As part of the ongoing efforts to improve student achievement, self-reflected processes such as protocols, fish bowls, and data analysis will be used to assess the effectiveness of performance.
- Remuneration will be performance based.
- The principal and staff will be recognized for innovative practices beyond the school site, that is, district, county, state, and national levels.
- Surveys from all, including students, will be part of the evaluation process.

(Continued)

TABLE 4.4
(Continued)

Self-Actualization

- "No quacking"
- Above and beyond

Evidence

_____

_____

_____

Instructional Strategies

Emerging

- Principal observes teacher and provides feedback on observed instructional strategies.
- Principal reads, analyzes, and discusses with teachers information on research-based practices that result in increased student achievement.
- Lesson design and instructional strategies are aligned with standards and assessments.

Applying

- Lesson design and instructional strategies are aligned with standards and assessments.
- Principal assists teachers in becoming effective instructional leaders by providing staff development and demonstrating instructional strategies that reflect best practices and result in increased student achievement.
- Principal holds teachers accountable for implementation of research-based practices to address needs of all students resulting in increased student achievement.

Innovating

- Principal holds teachers accountable for the implementation of differentiated educational learning plans with long- and short-term goals specific to each child, which may include virtual Web-based learning opportunities.
- The entire learning community team takes responsibility for each child's learning.

(Continued)

TABLE 4.4
(Continued)

Self-Actualization
- "No quacking"
- Above and beyond

Evidence

_____

_____

_____

Implementation of Change Process for Continuous Student Improvement

Emerging
- Principal identifies need for systemic change based on data collection, analysis, and inquiry.
- Principal investigates avenues of change with all stakeholders.
- Principal has the ability to communicate and prioritize information to facilitate the change process.

Applying
- Principal facilitates the implementation and maintenance of the change process with all stakeholders.
- Principal has the ability to articulate, implement, and demonstrate a unity of purpose.

Innovating
- As evidence of systemic change, all stakeholders have assumed responsibility and ownership for ensuring that school reform continues to meet the diverse needs of all students.

Self-Actualization
- "No quacking"
- Above and beyond

Evidence

_____

_____

_____

(Continued)

TABLE 4.4
(Continued)

Principal Standard No. 2: The principal is accountable for building leadership capacity.

Hire Personnel With Capacity to Do Leadership Work

Emerging
- Principal facilitates a process to select employees based on screening and interview only.
- Principal facilitates a process to select employees based on screening, interview, and observation of a teaching demonstration lesson.

Applying
- Principal facilitates a process to select employees based on screening, interview, and observation of a teaching demonstration lesson and has the candidate describe how he or she perceives his or her role as teacher, how he or she improves his or her craft of teaching.
- Principal uses simulations for candidates to interact in problem-solving activities and also asks candidate to respond to a case study.
- SRI Teacher Perceiver is a tool used during the interview process.
- Interview teams are trained as to what to look and listen for during an interview.

Innovating
- Principal is a connoisseur of talent, hires for attitude and trains for skill, and dares to collaborate and to hire based on values and dreams over experience and years of services.

Self-Actualization
- "No quacking"
- Above and beyond

Evidence

(Continued)

TABLE 4.4

(Continued)

Assess and Monitor Staff and School Capacity for Leadership

Emerging

- Principal surveys/observes staff for leadership capacity.
- Principal surveys/observes staff for leadership capacity and uses data to summarize staffs' highest needs.

Applying

- Principal assists staff in prioritizing and selecting options for participating in leadership opportunities and uses data to summarize staff's current leadership status.
- Principal provides time, resources, and opportunities for staff to chair committees, lead staff development, and participate in collaborative action research.
- Principal acknowledges staff for self-assessment and encourages active involvement of all stakeholders.

Innovating

- Principal uses multiple methods to develop leadership capacity for each teacher.
- Representatives of all stakeholders design the criteria for measuring staff and school capacity for leadership.
- An Individualized Leadership Growth Plan that includes activities that promote staff leadership beyond the school site and may include the SRI is developed.
- Leadership skills are focused on engaging reluctant staff and parents in leadership roles.

Self-Actualization

- "No quacking"
- Above and beyond

Evidence

_____

_____

_____

(Continued)

TABLE 4.4
(Continued)

Build Student, Parent, and Community Leadership

Emerging

- Principal encourages students, parents, and community members to participate in established organizations that require their involvement and encourages them to volunteer.
- Parents are actively recruited to participate in mandated committees, and their input is valued.
- Principal models community participation through membership in PTA/PTC, service clubs, and other community organizations.

Applying

- Parents, students, and community members are involved in all facets of the school governance structure and are a part of all student-based decision making.
- Parents, students, and community members represent the school in community and district organizations.
- Parents, students, and community members work with staff to present and facilitate community forums.

Innovating

- The principal collaborates with staff, students, and community to create a new service model that will meet all needs of students, their families, and the community, such as Spirit of Caring, or Healthy Start.
- There is a focus on providing services beyond the schoolhouse walls.

Self-Actualization

- "No quacking"
- Above and beyond

Evidence

_____

_____

_____

(Continued)

TABLE 4.4

(Continued)

Develop a Culture of Inquiry

Emerging

- Principal examines student work and analyzes data.
- Principal asks questions of staff that foster dialogue and reflection on data.

Applying

- Principal creates opportunity for stakeholders to develop a plan of action based on inquiry.
- Principal asks questions of staff that foster dialogue and reflection on data.
- Principal provides opportunities for examination of disaggregated data to reflect on instructional practices.
- Collaboratively, all stakeholders address areas of need, modify instructional practices, and provide for a review of resources.

Innovating

- Through the inquiry process, mistakes are viewed as learning tools and levers to the change process.
- Staff seeks input from community and "Critical Friends," that is, experts outside of the school site, to collaborate with them on supportive statements and critical questions.

Self-Actualization

- "No quacking"
- Above and beyond

Evidence

(Continued)

TABLE 4.4
(Continued)

Organize School Community for Collaborative Work

Emerging
- Principal shares decision making with small groups; that is, leadership team, School Site Council, PTA/PTC, and other governance groups.
- Principal responds reactively instead of proactively.

Applying
- Principal promotes and practices collaborative student-based decision making that provides options to meet diverse individual and group needs of the school community.
- Principal is proactive and participates in community service organizations.

Innovating
- To ensure student success, the entire learning community consistently seeks and collaborates with others to create new models that foster increased collaborative work.
- Staff and students give back to the community through service-oriented activities.

Self-Actualization
- "No quacking"
- Above and beyond

Evidence

_____

_____

_____

(Continued)

TABLE 4.4

(Continued)

Principal Standard No. 3: The principal is accountable for customer satisfaction.

School Culture

Emerging

- Principal is responsible for and collaborates with staff in establishing a culture that fosters mutual respect, fairness, pride, collegiality, trust, and excellence within the school community.
- Principal fosters a welcoming and inclusive atmosphere.
- Principal makes positive connections with students as demonstrated by their interactions with him or her.

Applying

- Principal takes responsibility for creating a student leadership team, representative of all, that develops an ongoing process to address student rights, hear student voices, and ensure student-based decision making.
- Principal fosters a welcoming and inclusive atmosphere for all staff, students, parents, and community.

Innovating

- The entire school community demonstrates a willingness to continuously examine assumptions, beliefs, and practices in doing the work required for high levels of personal and organizational performance.
- The school culture reflects a customer-driven environment.
- There is an established process for addressing problems and mediating conflict.

Self-Actualization
- "No quacking"
- Above and beyond

Evidence

(Continued)

TABLE 4.4
(Continued)

Communication

Emerging

- Principal communicates effectively, understanding the unique needs of community, and channels information in specialized ways to fit the traditions and expectations of community.
- Principal uses basic communication skills, for example, electronic mail.
- Principal listens and responds to selected stakeholders.

Applying

- Principal facilitates the effective flow of information to all customers to ensure a sound communication loop with all stakeholders, including Educational Services and Support Center (ESSC).
- Principal applies technology to magnify and enhance communication.
- Principal carefully plans, systematically manages, and continuously refines communication throughout the organization and between the school and its stakeholders.
- Principal applies active listening techniques to all stakeholders.
- Principal is the key communicator and is responsible for setting the tone of Aim Frame versus Blame Frame.
- Communication is proactive and timely.

Innovating

- Technology is used throughout the school community to magnify and enhance communication.
- There is a commitment to create opportunities for dialogue with parents, community members, business/service organizations, and colleagues.
- Concerns and issues are depersonalized and handled in an "Aim Frame" professional manner.

Self-Actualization

- "No quacking"
- Above and beyond

Evidence

(Continued)

TABLE 4.4
(Continued)

Parent Involvement

Emerging

- Principal communicates to all stakeholders respect for the important role parents play as partners in educating their children, which has a direct impact on student achievement.

Applying

- Principal instills the value of parent participation in the school and also models inclusiveness in his or her interactions with parents, staff, and students.
- As a result of principal leadership, all staff, parents, and community agree on a Home/School Contract that will be monitored by a panel of staff, community, and parents.

Innovating

- All stakeholders embrace the value of inclusion in all decision making.
- The school is the center of a learning community that provides parents requested services such as high school equivalency classes, English as a second language, training and utilization of technology, welfare to work program, and parenting classes.

Self-Actualization

- "No quacking"
- Above and beyond

Evidence

(Continued)

TABLE 4.4
(Continued)

Principal Standard No. 4: The principal is accountable for acting with integrity, fairness, and in an ethical and legal manner at all times.

Ethical Behavior

Emerging

- Principal actively demonstrates that students are the center of all decision making.
- Principal models professional responsibility with honesty, trust, and integrity and implements the governing board's policies and administrative rules and regulations.
- The principal supports, promotes, and models the district's vision and values at all times.

Applying

- Principal consistently facilitates the decision-making process with the well-being of students as the focus.
- Principal's behavior consistently reflects honesty and integrity as she or he implements the governing board's policies and administrative rules and regulations.

Innovating

- Principal demonstrates standards of exemplary professional conduct, with the well-being of students being the fundamental value of all decision making.
- All stakeholders are treated with respect and dignity, and all have an equal voice in student-based decision making.
- Decisions are made based on principles, not preferences.

Self-Actualization
- "No quacking"
- Above and beyond

Evidence

_____

_____

_____

(Continued)

TABLE 4.4
(Continued)

Shared Values

Emerging
- Principal refers to the vision and values, strategic goals, and student-based philosophy when reviewing the school plan.

Applying
- Principal makes a commitment to the vision and values, strategic goals, and student-based philosophy when reviewing the school plan on a consistent basis in dealings with students, parents, staff, and community.
- Vision, values, strategic goals, and philosophy are embodied in day-to-day operations.

Innovating
- Vision is implemented through action reflecting deep core values and beliefs.

Self-Actualization
- "No quacking"
- Above and beyond

Evidence

TABLE 4.4
(Continued)

Shared Decision Making

Emerging

- Under the leadership of the principal, a committee investigates a process for shared decision making.
- When shared decisions result in negative impact on children, the principal takes responsibility for leadership.

Applying

- A structure is established for shared decision making and can be articulated by all stakeholders.
- When shared decisions result in negative impact on children, there is prompt and honest action, and a willingness to accept responsibility for the decision made.
- The principal, through a process of evaluation, guides the shared decision-making process so results will have a positive impact on children.

Innovating

- Through cognition and instinct, the principal consistently implements the steps to good decision making and is able to accept blame without shame, learn the lessons that failure has to teach, and move on when a poor decision has been made.

Self-Actualization

- "No quacking"
- Above and beyond

Evidence

(Continued)

TABLE 4.4
(Continued)

Principal Standard No. 5: The principal is accountable for managing the school site as a safe, efficient, and effective learning environment.

Safety

Emerging

- Principal develops and implements schoolwide safety and discipline plans.
- Principal assesses need for safety and anticipates safety and discipline issues.
- All stakeholders understand the physical and emotional needs for safety, and the maintenance of the physical environment is sustained with a preventative eye.

Applying

- Principal makes student voice the cornerstone of all decision making and provides ongoing opportunities for all students to be heard regarding their physical and emotional safety; this process will result in positive student behavior and achievement.
- Principal uses data gathered from staff, parents, and students to monitor and implement the effectiveness of a schoolwide safety/discipline plan and works with staff to collaborate, refine, and improve schoolwide safety and student behavior.
- Everyone takes responsibility for the safety of all children.
- A variety of preventative interventions are established.

Innovating

- Discipline is a part of ongoing learning focused on self-actualization.
- Students are self-directed and make a safe learning environment a top priority as demonstrated by their actions.

Self-Actualization
- "No quacking"
- Above and beyond

Evidence

(Continued)

TABLE 4.4
(Continued)

Conflict Resolution

Emerging
- Principal demonstrates ability to facilitate and successfully resolve conflict at local level.
- Principal leads students, staff, and community in development of skills in problem solving and conflict resolution.
- Principal sees conflict and disequilibrium and manages it.

Applying
- Principal provides ongoing opportunities and establishes an infrastructure supporting student-based decision making, using learned mediation skills and processes.
- Principal successfully manages conflict in a proactive manner.
- Principal institutes a student conflict resolution coalition that promotes schoolwide peace, respect, and understanding.

Innovation
- Divergent opinions that create conflict are valued and treated with respect and dignity by all stakeholders.
- The principal seeks disequilibrium and creates conflict with purpose and meaning.

Self-Actualization
- "No quacking"
- Above and beyond

Evidence

_____

_____

_____

(Continued)

TABLE 4.4
(Continued)

Technology

Emerging

- Principal uses technology to effectively manage site data and generate district reports or information according to required district time lines.
- Principal monitors that students and staff are routinely utilizing technology as a tool for instruction.
- In collaboration with stakeholders, principal develops and implements a plan and demonstrates to staff how to integrate technology into the curriculum.

Applying

- Principal builds on staff and student strengths and community and student interests to move the school forward in the use of technology to generate school reports and student products and provides necessary staff development.
- Principal works with staff to utilize data to inform instruction.
- Technology is a tool used to magnify and enhance instruction.

Innovating

- Principal initiates the challenge of change in technology and creates models to motivate the staff and students to acquire the necessary skills to compete in the 21st century.
- Technology is utilized as a tool for learning and focused on instruction and achievement.
- The use of technology is seamless and unnoticed.

Self-Actualization

- "No quacking"
- Above and beyond

Evidence

(Continued)

TABLE 4.4
(Continued)

School Operations

Emerging

- Principal understands district and site budgets and uses them to meet long- and short-term instructional program goals.
- Principal understands the intent, rule, regulations, and limitations of appropriate categorically funded programs and provides for staff and community involvement in budget preparation.
- Principal maintains security and safety measures and oversees the daily care of the physical plant by working collaboratively with facilities, transportation, food services, and other appropriate ESSC departments.

Applying

- Principal demonstrates expertise in utilizing site budgets to meet long- and short-term instructional program goals.
- Principal actively seeks additional staff development in budget design and understanding by their participation in District Budget Committee, Association of California School Administrators' Business Managers Academy, and other budget-related in-services. Principal develops an inclusive budget process to involve all stakeholders.
- Principal collaborates with ESSC departments to maintain a secure and safe learning environment.

Innovating

- Principal assumes responsibility and is accountable for implementation of a direct-funded model.
- Principal facilitates a process that involves all stakeholders in budget decision making.
- Principal works with the ESSC and makes decisions that will not negatively impact others.
- Principal creates an environment that enables staff to choose alternatives to employee representation.
- Principal shares expertise and provides assistance outside the school walls.

Self-Actualization
- "No quacking"
- Above and beyond

Evidence

_____

_____

_____

story is that you can quack like ducks and stay behind, or you can soar with eagles.

The question is, which do you want to be? "No quacking" is the principals' mantra. Leadership involves action and risk taking but also common sense.

WHAT IMPACT DOES "NEW BLOOD" HAVE ON THE ORGANIZATION?

The 1999–2000 school year brought seven new principals into the group. Even though there was apprehension and some trepidation about "new blood," the new principals' enthusiasm and positive response to the Principal Standards' draft energized the group and led all of the principals to adopt the current working document. The evolution continues as the new principals and the other principals work together within their peer groups and begin the journey of trust.

To illustrate the process used in the Principal Peer Evaluation, refer to Figure 4.2. Note that the appraisal documentation form used for principal peer evaluation has a column with performance weights. These refer to the percentage of value placed on that standard. The standard is weighted differently for first-time principals and new principals. Details relating to each standard within the continuum framework are described in Table 4.4. Figure 4.3 is the worksheet used during the performance evaluation.

The missing component of the evaluation is the determination of merit pay. Principals created a structure for performance-based compensation using the Principal Standards as its foundation. After much rich discussion and examination of other bonus pay formats, such as the one used by the Edison Schools Incorporated, the principals agreed to a weighted plan. This topic continues to create philosophical dissonance. During the pilot year, participation in performance-based compensation was voluntary.

Principal peer groups are becoming more familiar with the Principal Standards working document and are identifying areas within each standard on which individuals are to focus. The principals of the district are truly pioneers in the realm of principal peer-evaluation redesign. Although some continue to be skeptical, most are willing to

Figure 4.2. Principal Performance Appraisal, 1999–2000 Year

School _____ Principal _____

Content Standards (aligned with Principal Performance Standards document)

Principal Standards	Weight[a] PY1 PY2+	Self-Reflection[b]	Peer Reflection[c]	Super-intendent/ Cabinet[d]	Appraisal Score[e]	Weighted Appraisal Score[f]
Student Achievement	.25 (.50)					
Building Leadership Capability	.25 (.30)					
Customer Satisfaction	.20 (.075)					
Legal and Ethical Responsibility	.15 (.075)					
Safe Learning Environment	.15 (.05)					
					TOTAL SCORE	[g]

KEY:

Summary Appraisals	*Report Card and Appraisal Scores*	*Summary Appraisal Ranges*
Does Not Meet Expectations	1	1.00-1.49
Approaching Expectations	2 (Emerging)	1.50-2.49
Meets Expectations	3 (Applying)	2.50-3.49
Exceeds Expectations	4 (Innovating)	3.50-4.00

a. The term PY1 refers to performance year one. This includes first-time principals or experienced principals assigned to a new site. The term PY2 refers to performance year two and above.
b. Individual reflective self-reports and ratings.
c. Peer-group ratings based on group discussions and data.
d. Superintendent/cabinet ratings based on data observations and team consensus.
e. Total of ratings (using scale identified in KEY)
f. Product by multiplying columns 5 and 1.
g. Total score aligned with bonus pay (see Figure 4.3).

Figure 4.3. Chula Vista Elementary School District, Worksheet for Principal Bonuses/
Merit Pay, 1999–2000

School: _____

Principal: _____

Available Bonus: _____$10,000_____

Total Appraisal Score: _____

Bonus Percentage Earned: _____

Bonus Awarded: _____

Appraiser's Signature: _____ Date: _____

Principal's Signature: _____ Date: _____

1.00-1.49:	0%	2.30-2.39:	0%	3.20-3.29:	20%
1.50-1.59:	0%	2.40-2.49:	0%	3.30-3.39:	30%
1.60-1.69:	0%	2.50-2.59:	0%	3.40-3.49:	40%
1.70-1.79:	0%	2.60-2.69:	0%	3.50-3.59:	50%
1.80-1.89:	0%	2.70-2.79:	0%	3.60-3.69:	60%
1.90-1.99:	0%	2.80-2.89:	0%	3.70-3.79:	70%
2.00-2.09:	0%	2.90-2.99:	0%	3.80-3.89:	80%
2.10-2.19:	0%	3.00-3.09:	0%	3.90-3.99:	90%
2.20-2.29:	0%	3.10-3.19:	10%	4.00-4.00+	100%

participate in this opportunity for growth. Inherent in all redesign efforts are various levels of acceptance. The following quotes illustrate the present level of thinking and reflect the variety of opinions among principals and their acceptance of this bold, innovative change process.

Previous evaluation model—looks good on paper? Peer evaluation—you better walk the walk and put your money where your mouth is.

I appreciate the process of receiving feedback from my peers, and I am excited by the notion of compensation for my hard and "courageous" work. My biggest fear relates to the time commitment involved in the process (especially if we are going to do it "well") in light of the time demands already inherent in the job.

I also think that it is quite likely that a principal who receives a bonus will find it to be a detriment to the team approach that allowed the principal to receive the bonus. I also think that it makes no sense to assume that a principal will suddenly unleash heretofore unused administrative skills to make a few thousand extra.

I do look to the future with some fear because I know that I have a lot to learn. Accomplishing school reform in the superintendent's time frame is difficult. Moving the school organization with all of the anxiety that a lot of change creates is hard to accomplish in a short time frame.

The peer evaluation groups are evolving into communities of learners. Together, we are studying standards that have been set forth for our students and staffs. This has resulted in the development of principal standards.

With the standards for principals, we have another vehicle for motivating growth and development. To receive recognition (bonus pay) for growth would be very gratifying.

I think by opening it up to peers, it greatly expands the ideas and methods. However, I am concerned about the added responsibility of peer evaluations when our responsibilities are so vast at this time.

I will invite my peers to ask the difficult questions of me to frame my self-reflection and to help me formulate my goals.

BOX 4.2

What Does the Board Say About Principal Standards?

"Principal standards are a must if you want your district to perform at its highest level. . . . When you have principal standards, all . . . know what is expected . . . and you have a way of monitoring progress. The peer evaluation model can be a very productive method of motivating administrators."

"The principal standards are a beginning process to hold administrators accountable. By following the standards, we will see more principals willing to make changes."

I do what I do because I love it. I care about children. I love teaching. I think we all share in our successes as well as our failures. Of course, I would hope to receive a bonus, since it is the mechanism that has been established to recognize our efforts.

The process has been fair, orderly, and, for the most part, pretty well thought through to this point. Within a year or two, however, we should know if it has been effective, made a difference, and [was] worth the time and energy put into this project.

The journey from peer group autonomy to the establishment of standards as an evaluation tool is a rigorous, long, challenging process that continues to evolve on a daily basis. Throughout this process, the cabinet and the board remain in strong support.

The principal has the power to facilitate or block change efforts. The messages s/he sends formally and informally about what is important have profound effects on the school's culture, climate, programs, and people. As Sergiovanni (1987) and others have pointed out, the ability of leaders to communicate their values and beliefs to others in a way that provides context and meaning is highly significant in the life of a school.

Boston, 1991, p. 88

Lessons Learned and Beyond

5

Principals look to the future of the peer-evaluation process and the Principal Standards for Accountability as they welcome new challenges and embrace opportunities to redefine their roles. As the world continues its rapid pace of change, principals strive to achieve the self-actualization level of the Principal Standards (Chapter 4). It is not clearly delineated. The definition of self-actualization is envisioned and shaped continually by empowered and forward-thinking leaders at each school site. In fact, the very term *self-actualization* is future oriented and is therefore perpetually and intentionally undefined.

Whereas some districts are recentralizing decisions, Chula Vista Elementary School District principals are given autonomy with responsibility to create learning environments that foster increased student achievement. With this empowerment comes accountability, and principals in this district are responding to the strong sense of urgency to better prepare students for a world not yet foreseen.

Previous chapters describe the principals' and the district's journey; the dance has just begun. There are more questions than answers.

> Educational leadership involves many dimensions focusing on accountability, including but not limited to academic achievement, community involvement, fiscal responsibility, personnel management, and the development of a shared inspirational vision to which all stakeholders respond.
>
> *Principal, Chula Vista Elementary School District*

Issues remain for this district. Trust continues to be an ongoing concern. As in many organizations, there is a "good old boys" network challenging a group of leaders untethered by past politics and eager for a new vision.

Willingness to reflect honestly, share insights, and accept the criticism of peers requires a degree of confidence in the skills and integrity of colleagues. This may, in part, be an issue of ego; however, it also involves the same type of confidence a dancer would need while performing Swan Lake. Stephen Covey states, "Effective interdependence can only be built on a foundation of true independence. Private victory precedes public victory" (p. 185). An essential issue for each principal is the understanding of personal accomplishments within the district as well as at the individual school site.

As the level of trust increases and principals learn to give critical feedback and develop skills to evaluate colleagues, the power of the peer-review process will be realized. Principals are skilled at assessing progress of students, teachers, programs, curriculum, and support personnel; however, to apply a measurement to one's peers requires self-examination.

According to Gerry House (1999), Superintendent of Memphis City Schools, "we have conquered many new frontiers, the most important of which is the unmined intellect of our children. This is indeed a territory worth fighting for. Principals are committed to a positive, stimulating learning environment for all children—one that prepares them for a new era" (p. 38).

LESSONS PRINCIPALS ARE LEARNING

The change process can be painful. This is particularly true of the essential changes required of today's principals. Communities demand increased student learning at all levels requiring new and innovative ideas and practices. Principals must accept the need to reevaluate current practices and to check their egos at the door. They must learn new skills and be accountable for increased academic achievement. Finally, principals must adopt innovative ideas such as principal performance standards and peer evaluations, which may have undefined goals.

With change comes disequilibrium. Feelings of frustration and confusion are rampant. The feeling is not unlike learning a new dance. The music might be familiar, but moving your body in new and different ways causes you momentarily to miss the beat entirely. Principals learn that having perseverance and flexibility is imperative during this transition. They learn to depend on each other not only for expertise but also for moral support.

Principals must have an internal locus of control. Leaders and change agents must develop a sense of urgency. It is no longer an acceptable practice to wait for direction from above. Principals must stop looking outside the system for root causes for lack of student achievement. They must stay focused on solutions and model the behaviors and attitudes they wish to see manifested in their constituencies. Core values and beliefs must drive decisions to benefit children.

Trust comes before honesty. Change in an organization requires trust. This trust needs to be nourished and promoted. To get to honest self-reflection, trust must be a practicing core value. This is an ongoing challenge as peer-group members change and new hires join the leadership team. Trust must be conscientiously developed and explicitly fostered to support the forward movement of an organization.

Data, data, data. There is new public awareness about the importance of data. It is no longer acceptable to make blanket statements and unsubstantiated conclusions. Research-based information carries more weight. Consumers are reading labels, including the fine print. Therefore, principal evaluations must now also be supported by data such as student test scores, staff/student/parent surveys, student attendance patterns, and other measurable information. This is an integral component of the evaluation process used by the Chula Vista Elementary School District. Benchmarks are identified, and goals are set. Data are essential in performance measurement for adults as well as for children.

Political implications are drivers of the change process. Current legislative education reform efforts have focused particularly on the leadership role of the school principal, thus implying a change from traditional practices. One hypothesis that is being tested assumes that empowering local schools with greater autonomy and resources will result in greater accountability for student outcomes. New leadership must initiate and accept responsibility.

In the process of principal evaluation, autonomy becomes essential for effective leadership. Principals discover that when individuals work in isolation, without a shared purpose or common vision, this affects their ability to address student needs effectively. The procedures and materials mandated by local, state, and federal officials do not bring about appropriate change—educational leaders do.

> We live in a time of paradigm shifts. Not everyone can formulate successful, new paradigms. Only a few do that. But all of us can be more open to looking for the changes, exploring them for their implications, and creating a supporting climate for the attempts. There is no question that, in many cases, we need new paradigms. In ever increasing frequency, the call for innovation goes out across the United States, and around the globe. Paradigm shifts are one of the key innovative behaviors.
>
> *Barker, 1992, p. 207*

NEXT STEPS

After three years of writing, rewriting, discussing, and revising the Principal Standards and the Peer Evaluation Process, there are still questions and concerns regarding the process and its value in pro-

---

Figure 5.1. Expectations of Principal Institute Sessions

- Raising the bar for expectations and accountability

- Committing to regularly scheduled professional development training

- Using the inquiry process to challenge and promote group thinking

- Reflecting continuously on new ideas

---

moting the success of the principal. The challenge is to continually revisit both concerns with critical lenses. The Principal Performance Standards are the vehicle of continued professional growth and cause us to reflect on our practices.

To address the collective understanding of Principal Performance Standards, an external facilitator has come in to work with all the principals. Peer groups conducted a number of activities around the Principal Performance Standards to clarify understandings and the need for revisions. This session was the first in a proposed series of work sessions to revise and refine the original Principal Performance Standards document to align with the district (see Figure 5.1).

The facilitator will also work with principals to calibrate a rating scale related to bonus pay. The goal of these work sessions is to bring clarity, understanding, and consensus. Here are some questions we ask ourselves as we look to the future:

Do we have the courage to suspend judgment as we redefine the future?

How can we expand our vision of schooling and learning to incorporate unknown technological advances?

Our "big toe" is out of the box. How will we sustain the momentum to respond to and create the future?

How will we harness the dissonance of change as an energizing force?

How do we ensure that all children have equal access and equity?

Our new way of working is just at its beginning. Collectively, we will continue to be lifetime learners and creators of an educational system that enriches and energizes the learning lives of our children. This book is written in the spirit of placing the principal in the position to best create a learning community. It is the authors' hope that readers will continue this work and expand it. We will continue to use and modify this model, and we hope that others will follow our lead. Knowing that this is truly a journey that we take together, we challenge other principals to look outside the box and improve the status of the children in schools. We ask that you share your challenges as well as your successes.

Appendix A:

Demographic Background and Article on Principals Evaluating Peers

District Demographics: The Chula Vista Elementary School District (web page: www.cvesd.k12.ca.us) is the largest K–6 District in the state of California, serving more than 22,250 students in 37 schools during the 1999–2000 school year. The district is located between the city of San Diego and the United States–Mexico international border, covering 103 square miles in the fastest growing region in San Diego County. The ethnic background of students is

60.0%	Hispanic
22.5%	White
7.2%	Filipino
5.4%	African American
3.4%	Asian
.8%	Pacific Islander
.7%	Native American

In addition to English and Spanish, about 45 different home languages have been identified. Recognizing the diverse needs of students and communities, the Chula Vista Elementary School District offers a variety of program models, which include five charter schools, accelerated schools project, Comer school development program, Healthy Start/Family Resource Centers, direct instruction, and magnet schools for science and the visual and performing arts. A commitment to collaborative efforts has resulted in numerous partnerships: U.S. Navy, Saturday Scholars Program; Sharp and Scripps Hospitals, Mobile Pediatric Clinic; Olympic Training Center, Exercise the Dream Program; Chula Vista Nature Center, Young Scientists Program; and many more at individual school sites.

In the following article, Superintendent Libia S. Gil describes the principal peer-evaluation program. It is reprinted from the December 1998 issue with permission of *The School Administrator* magazine.

BY LIBIA S. GIL

Principals
Evaluating Peers

T he word "evaluation" evokes a variety of responses dictated by personal experiences with the process. Often the mechanistic procedure is simply viewed as a necessary chore to complete for both the evaluator and evaluatee.

In fall 1993, as the new superintendent of the Chula Vista Elementary School District, in Chula Vista, Calif., I conducted an individual assessment of the organization with each principal. Thirty-two principals provided their insights on strengths and areas for improvement. The top three issues quickly surfaced, and the principals' evaluation process was on that list.

The principals here shared deep concerns that the existing evaluation process was a "dog-and-pony show" with little or no relevance to their leadership performance, their improvement and student achievement. Under this system, principals presented individual goals and objectives annually to all cabinet members. Subsequently, they would be evaluated by different assistant superintendents who had differing standards and expectations. Some principals believed that competition between the two assistant superintendents distorted their efforts so the focus became who could produce the best

How one school district is developing leadership capacity to assume full responsibility for student growth

video, portfolio or presentation by the end of the year.

Many principals candidly admitted they fabricated observation data for submission to their supervisor. To gain approval, principals sent documents to comply with central-office dictates with no qualitative review and feedback. Recording activities and keeping track of participation in events had taken on its own value because no attempt was made to connect these actions to outcomes. Individual principals were jumping hoops to please central-office administrators with little or no accountability for leadership's impact on staff and student performance.

During the 1993-1994 school year, a principal task force was formed to review literature and research on evaluation models. At the time, we discovered many peer models for teachers but none designed for principals. We studied several interesting evaluation processes and instruments (Louisville, Ky., Seattle, Wash., and Vancouver, Wash.) and incorporated various components to create our own.

Promoting Growth

We spent considerable time defining the purpose of an evaluation process. We agreed that the primary purpose of an evaluation process is to promote professional and personal growth and development. We agreed that an effective evaluation process is ongoing and open and reflects honest communication, pointing to the importance of sharing concerns and critical feedback immediately to avoid surprises.

In addition, the philosophy of multiple assessments for performance status needs to apply to adults as well as students. Regular surveys of community, parents, staff and students are conducted and feedback is considered seriously and incorporated for improvement actions. Longitudinal student achievement data as well as attendance rates and other school profile data also is considered in

the feedback process. This shifts the focus on making a difference for student results by *doing* in contrast to *recording* activities for compliance.

Our Procedures

Changes in the evaluation process were implemented in 1994-1995. All 35 principals now report directly to the superintendent. Peer groups were formed through self-selection with consideration of common goals, geographic representation, size, diversity and relationships. Peer group sizes range from four to seven members and meet monthly throughout the school year.

Each principal has an initial conference with the superintendent followed by group goal-setting sessions. The group selects a common focus based on predetermined criterion. (The peer groups use performance indicators in professional growth, school improvement, evaluation of school personnel, management, communication and community relations.) Throughout the process, it is important that individual concerns or personnel issues remain confidential between the principal and the superintendent unless the principal chooses to divulge.

Each peer group identifies individuals to be evaluated on a two-year rotation cycle with the exception of new principals who must submit annual evaluations for a three-year probationary period. Peer group evaluations do not preclude the superintendent's role and responsibility in holding individuals accountable for their leadership behaviors and implementing plans for

improvement when necessary.

The peer groups use an array of approaches to observe, learn and provide feedback to each principal. These include classroom observations, analysis of student work, formal interviews with key staff and parent leaders and regular meetings to solve problems and exchange ideas. Peer sessions also provide a measure of catharsis.

At the end of the first year, group conferences with the superintendent address these two questions: What did we learn? What difference has it made (if any) on my leadership ability to improve student learning?

Two-Year Assessment

In fall 1996, principals assessed the strengths and weaknesses of the peer group evaluation process.

Among the strengths, they reported the following:
- valued interactions with other principals because they led to new relationships and friendships;
- found support and assistance for dealing with difficult issues;
- gained diverse perspectives and varied expertise;
- brainstormed solutions to common and uncommon problems;
- built trust through frequent non-threatening, candid communication with a core group; and
- established meaningful evaluation through learning and cooperative efforts.

They pointed to these weaknesses:
- lack of enough time to visit and process information;
- lack of consistency in that expectations are not clearly defined; and
- reluctance to offer criticism.

The principals offered several suggestions for improving the peer review process. These included the need to clearly articulate expectations among the group members; to designate one meeting per month for principal peer groups; and to share procedures among groups.

An Evolving Process

The Peer Group Evaluation Process has evolved to a higher level of expectations that are generated internally and externally. Most peer groups have taken advantage of the opportunity to strengthen their leadership impact with ongoing dialogues and supportive critiques.

Focus Questions for Peer Groups

As superintendent, I provide focus questions for the principals in their peer groups to consider each year. These mirror the school district's shared vision, values and goals.

Examples include:

How have you raised expectations for students, staff and self?

How have you demonstrated teamwork for student success?

During 1997-98 year, the focus questions were:

How are you using data to improve

your instructional program?

(Principals were asked to consider longitudinal cohorts, findings from surveys conducted in our community by pollster Gordon Black, portfolios, report cards and school profiles.)

What changes will you make in your role as an instructional leader?

(Principals were to consider their own performance as well as performance of teachers and students.)

How will the peer group assist you in achieving goals 1 and 2?

— Libia Gil

Principal Jane Litchko (left) of Jackson Road Elementary School in Adelphi, Md., meets with teachers.

Although relationships within groups are strong and each group has established a foundation of trust, transfer to the group-at-large has been minimal. Intergroup dynamics continue to fluctuate as a result of professional rivalry, intolerance and resistance to changing the status quo. In addition, we must reinforce questions about accountability and a continuous focus on data-driven, student-based decision making.

The peer evaluation process has provided an effective structure for continuous principal support, allowing the superintendent and assistant superintendents to focus on individuals with the greatest needs. Linking leadership effectiveness and student achievement remains a priority and a challenge for accurate assessment.

Over the past five years, 13 principals have been placed on plans of improvement and six have gone on to become successful principals in the district.

The ongoing issues are these:

● how best to accomplish higher performance levels for our students and staff; and

● how best to develop leadership capacity that assumes responsibility for student growth and development.

The following excerpt from a recent report from one of the peer groups nicely captures the value of this process:

"The group agreed that the process of peer evaluation is both positive and risk taking. Used appropriately, the group can select coaches and mentors. Members also have immediate access to the experience and advice of colleagues with whom we can solve problems, brainstorm issues and receive constructive feedback on actions contemplated or taken.

"The process forces us to expand our professional repertoire, particularly because of the responsibility to bring something of value to the group to expand the knowledge of the group and to focus on student achievement with colleagues of like purpose. The peer evaluation process makes us responsible to and for providing competent leaders in education."

Libia Gil is superintendent of the Chula Vista Elementary School District, 84 East J St., Chula Vista, Calif. 91910-6199. E-mail:lgil@cvesd.K12.ca.edu

What Do Principals Think of Peer Review?

What do principals in Chula Vista, Calif., think about their peer evaluation process? Here are some selected views from six principals that were provided at the end of the 1997-98 school year.

● *Sam Snyder, 27-year principal:* "A real strength was in being at each other's sites ... and sharing specific ideas from that site, such as evaluation techniques, playground tournament concepts, staff discipline or monitoring ideas. Principals, by the nature of their job, are isolated from their peers; this program was a real boost toward gaining support from and for each other. I can't tell you how high the morale has soared since we have been in our group."

● *John Harder, 11-year principal:* "The most beneficial aspect of peer groups, in my opinion, was the development of trust so that participants could reveal themselves and share. When a problem occurred for one principal, it could be brought to the group and collegially examined towards a positive solution. ... Successes are also shared and freely given to others to copy without any feeling that someone is showing off ... Self-reflection and sharing with the team resulted in a different and more practical emphasis as contrasted with the past when principals gave a presentation or more passively met with their evaluator to receive their perceptions."

● *Pete Matz, 7-year principal:* "The process is extremely valuable and effective in encouraging and enabling principals to 'think outside of the box' and stretch their expectations for themselves. We're constantly swapping ideas, duplicating and expanding each other's successes. ... [The process] encourages us to share our mistakes as well as our accomplishments."

● *Larry Tagle, 1st-year principal:* "As a new principal, I found the Peer Group Evaluation Process very helpful. Not only was I able to get feedback and assistance on a regular basis, but I extended the process. ... This is a great mentoring process where we learn from each other."

● *Marge Grigsby, 5-year principal:* "The most significant impact of peer evaluation has been the creation of a climate of collaboration rather than competition. When we get together as a group, we discuss common issues and use our collective expertise to come up with solutions. ... We have moved past the stage of recognizing only successes to identifying areas of concern."

● *Edwardo Aceves, 23-year principal:* "This peer evaluation goes one step further than just providing a process for evaluation—it provides an ongoing learning experience for all participating administrators. The final result does not, as in the MBO lockstep method, become some type of meaningless written tripe that is submitted to a supervisor who does less reading of it than weighting of it to see if the abundant documentation meets the established criteria of 'busy work' (for the evaluatee), a meaningless paper chase (for the evaluator) and an experience devoid of any learning or substantive result."

Appendix B:

Elementary Principal Job Posting

The following document is a brochure published by the Chula Vista Elementary School District describing the position of Elementary Principal.

Chula Vista Elementary School District

San Diego County, California

You Are Invited to Apply
for the Position of

ELEMENTARY PRINCIPAL

CHULA VISTA ELEMENTARY SCHOOL DISTRICT

As the largest kindergarten through grade six school district in the state, the Chula Vista Elementary School District has a population of more than 22,000 students housed in 37 schools, including five Charter schools. The District covers 103 square miles and serves a diverse population that includes more than 180,000 people in the areas of Chula Vista, Bonita, EastLake, Sunnyside, and South San Diego. Fifteen schools are on a single-track, year-round calendar. One school is on a four-track calendar and one is on an extended year calendar. The remaining 20 schools are on the traditional year calendar.

CHULA VISTA COMMUNITY

The Chula Vista community is noted for its strong support of our District's schools. The Community recently approved a General Obligation Bond of $95 million by 76% of the vote. Plans are being finalized for health and safety improvments and the initiation of needed repairs and renovations at every school site.

Chula Vista has a population of 154,869 and is located between the City of San Diego and the United States/Mexico International Border. San Diego Bay is the western boundary of the city. The community is primarily residential with many parks, golf courses, a marina, a Nature Center, and an Olympic Training Center. A large number of colleges and universities are within easy driving distance. Many military facilities and research centers as well as electronic and other industries are located in the area.

San Diego County offers outstanding recreational activities including boating, fishing, professional football and baseball, the world-famous San Diego Zoo, Wild Animal Park, Balboa Park, and Sea World. Cultural opportunities include art galleries, museums, theaters, symphonies, and opera in a city with a rich historical background.

BOARD OF EDUCATION

Larry Cunningham, Sharon Giles
Patrick A. Judd, Bertha J. López, Pamela B. Smith

SUPERINTENDENT

Libia S. Gil, Ph.D.

Culturally Diverse and Bilingual Candidates are Encouraged to Apply

Qualifications

Applicants must have the following attributes:

STUDENT ADVOCATE ACCOUNTABLE
HIGH INTEGRITY COLLABORATIVE
VISION CHANGE AGENT
ENERGETIC INSTRUCTIONAL LEADER
EMPATHETIC COMPASSIONATE
EFFECTIVE COMMUNICATOR

- Expertise in curriculum, instruction, and assessment.

- Vision of educational excellence for all students aligned with the District's Vision and Values Statements.

- Expertise in shared decision making and sensitivity to the needs and concerns of teachers, classified employees, parents, and community members.

- High visibility in the community with an open door policy.

- Commitment to cooperation and collaboration with a proactive management style that supports shared decision making.

- Ability to promote an atmosphere for employees that enhances professional satisfaction and trust.

- Ability to effectively meet the needs of a diverse student population and school community, build on the strength of that diversity, and promote appreciation for all cultures.

- Understanding the process of systemic change and how to be a change agent.

- Ability to motivate and inspire others and to encourage innovation, creative thinking, and risk taking on behalf of all students.

- Experience which demonstrates the ability to manage finances and seek resources. Business/entrepeneur experience and interest.

- High tolerance for stress and ambiguity with the ability to function well under chaos of the change process.

- Technological and data analysis experience.

Process

Application Procedure

Interested candidates must submit or have forwarded to Human Resources the following: (Position is open until filled)

- Application
- Cover letter which addresses specific competencies for the position
- Current Resume
- Placement File
- Response to Focus Questions
- At least three Confidential Recommendation Forms
- Optional Portfolio

Requirements

- California Administrative Credential
- Master's Degree in School Administration highly desirable
- Evidence of successful experience as an elementary teacher
- Knowledge of language acquisition theory and practices and demonstrate sensitivity and understanding of working in a diverse, multicultural and multiethnic student and community environment
- Bilingual preferred

Salary

$81,000 to $86,000 plus excellent fringe benefits (207 days)

All inquiries and applications are to be referred to:

Richard T. Werlin
Assistant Superintendent, Human Resources
84 East J Street
Chula Vista, California 91910
Telephone: (619) 425-9600, ext. 1340
FAX: (619) 427-3271
E-Mail: rwerlin@cvesd.k12.ca.us
Web Site: http://www.cvesd.k12.ca.us

Glossary

Blame Frame/Aim Frame: This term was coined by Peter Stark of Peter Stark Associates to describe changing behaviors from blaming and complaining to aiming for success.

BRI (John's Basic Reading Inventory):   The Basic Reading Inventory is an individually administered informal reading test. It is used districtwide as pre- and posttest for reading comprehension and vocabulary development.

Cabinet: Consists of the superintendent, assistant superintendent of business services, assistant superintendent for human resources, and assistant superintendent for instructional services and support.

CHAT (Chula Vista Assistance Team):   Consists of selected certificated staff members whose job is to mentor teachers new to the district. The selection of CHAT colleagues is based on recognized excellence, expertise, and professionalism. Typically, new teachers receive this support during their first 2 years of service. The principals' group adopted this model and extended it to provide support to all principals.

EMI (The Elementary Mathematics Initiative) Assessment: A performance-based test that was developed by the California Math Consortium as an assessment in math computation and application for kindergarten through sixth grade.

Gordon-Black surveys (renamed Harris Interactive):   A district-wide survey administered to students, parents, community, staff, and administrators to determine attitudes and opinions regarding programs and procedures.

Locus of Control (LOC):   Attributions to either external factors or internal factors for one's success or failure.

SARB (School Attendance Review Board):   This is a multiagency committee that addresses critical attendance issues districtwide. Agencies include a district administrator, a district nurse, and representatives from the Probation Department, Child Protective Services, the Department of Social Services, Vista Hill Psychiatric Hospital, Children's Hospital, the Police Department, and the school principal. The committee meets to address issues related to truancy and to develop a plan with the parents and children to ensure consistent on-time attendance at school.

SAT⁹ (Stanford Achievement Test, 9th edition):   This is the assessment tool selected by the state of California to measure the success of each school's academic program.

Student-Based Decision Making: A process in which all decisions made at the school site maintain the focus of impact on students.

References

Barker, J. A. (1992). *Future edge: Discovering new paradigms of success.* New York: William Morrow.

Belasco, J. (1991). *Teaching the elephant to dance: The manager's guide to empowering change.* New York: Plume.

Black, S. (2000, September). Finding time to lead. *American School Board Journal,* pp. 46-48.

Boston, J. (1991). *Global education: From thought to action.* Alexandria, VA: Association for Supervision and Curriculum Development.

California Commission on Teacher Credentialing and the California Department of Education. (1997). *California standards for the teaching profession—July 1997.* Sacramento: Authors.

Covey, S. (1989). *The 7 habits of highly effective people.* New York: Simon & Schuster.

Dufour, R., & Eaker, R. (1991). *Creating the new American school: A principal's guide to school improvement.* Washington, DC: National Educational Service.

Dufour, R., & Eaker, R. (1992). *Creating the new American school.* Bloomington, IN: National Educational Service.

Frase, L. E., Downey, C. J., & Canciamilla, L. (1999, June). Putting principals in their place: The classroom. *Thrust,* pp. 36-39.

House, G. (1999). A simple choice: Change or boil to death. *The School Administrator,* pp. 36-38.

Ramsey, R. (1999). *Lead, follow, or get out of the way: How to be a more effective leader in today's schools.* Thousand Oaks, CA: Corwin.

Schlechty, P. C. (1990). *Schools for the 21st century: Leadership imperatives for educational reform.* San Francisco: Jossey-Bass.

Senge, P. (1999). *The dance of change: The challenges to sustaining momentum in learning organizations.* New York: Doubleday.

SUGGESTED READINGS

In conducting research for the principal peer group process, we found several published works useful in developing the plan. In addition to the works listed as references, which were mentioned in the text of our book, the following helped to frame our thoughts and elicit inquiry into peer evaluation and the scope of leadership across a spectrum of careers.

Aguayo, R. (1990). *Dr. Deming: What every U.S. business-person should know about successful management and bringing quality back home.* New York: Simon & Schuster.

Allen, R., & Allen, S. (1995). *Winnie-the-Pooh on problem solving: In which Pooh, Piglet, and friends explore how to solve problems so you can too.* New York: Dutton.

Blanchard, K. (1999). *The heart of a leader: Insights on the art of influence.* Tulsa, OK: Honor Books.

Blanchard, K., Hybels, B., & Hodges, P. (1999). *Leadership by the book: Tools to transform your workplace.* New York: William Morrow.

Cohen, W. A. (1990). *The art of the leader.* Englewood, NJ: Prentice Hall.

Crainer, S. (1999). *The 75 greatest management decisions ever made . . . And 21 of the worst.* New York: Amacom.

Crosby, P. (1996). *The absolutes of leadership.* San Francisco: Jossey-Bass.

DePree, M. (1992). *Leadership jazz.* New York: Dell.

Drucker, P. F. (1993) *The effective leader.* New York: Harper Business.

Fogg, C. D. (1994). *Team-based strategic planning: A complete guide to structuring, facilitating, and implementing the process.* New York: Amacom.

George, S., & Weimerskirch, A. (1994). *Total quality management: Strategies and techniques proven at today's most successful companies.* New York: John Wiley.

Gil, L. S. (1998, October). Principals evaluating peers. *The School Administrator,* pp. 28-30.

Grote, D. (1996). *The complete guide to performance appraisal.* New York: Amacom.

Hesselbein, F., & Cohen, P. (1999). *Leader to leader: Enduring insights on leadership from the Drucker Foundation Journal.* San Francisco: Jossey-Bass.

Johns, J. (1997). *Basic reading inventory.* Kendall Hunt.

Mackie, J. L. (1977). *Ethics: Inventing right and wrong.* New York: Penguin.

Oakley, E., & Krug, D. (1991). *Enlightened leadership: Getting to the heart of change.* New York: Fireside.

Shore, L. (1997). *Common purposes.* New York: Anchor Doubleday.

Yukl, G. (1998). *Leadership in organizations* (4th ed.). New York: Prentice Hall.

Index